後疫情時代的股市趨勢分析和投資建議

陳喬泓
張皓傑
葉芷娟
股海老牛

〈後疫情時代的股市趨勢分析和投資建議〉（1）

從長線來思考，現在是買點，絕非賣點！

陳喬泓

　　2022年上半年在俄烏戰爭、通膨快速飆升、聯準會升息縮表等利空因素下，全球股市皆呈現回跌走勢，台股也不例外，加權指數在年初來到18619點歷史高點後一路下殺，指數一度跌破萬四大關，最低來到13928點，波段累積跌幅高達25%，今年上半年合計跌3393點，為1990年後上半年最大跌點。

・加權指數上半年累積跌幅高達25%

　　當指數從高點計算跌幅逾兩成時，代表股市正式進入空頭走勢，根據過去歷史資料顯示，從1990年至今，台股總共經歷10次空頭市場，最少跌23%，最多跌65%（2000年網路

泡沫），平均跌幅約39%；最快3個月止跌（2020年新冠疫情）、最久整整跌了一年8個月，平均空頭時間接近一年（11個多月）。

不過就在俄烏戰爭結束之日仍遙遙無期，美國6月消費者物價指數（CPI）年增9.1%，再創逾40年來新高，Fed考慮升息4碼，恐使美國經濟陷入衰退等利空衝擊下，股市頻創新低，市場投資人信心已全面潰散之際，國安基金宣布進場護盤。

根據2008年以來國安基金護盤紀錄顯示，雖然短期勝率並非百分之百，也不排除在宣布進場後還有再跌一段的可能性，**但從長線來看，可以確定國安基金選擇進場的時機點，都是指數的相對低點**，只要投資人有耐心放一年以上，都有超過三成以上的上漲空間。

就在國安基金宣布進場不久後，台積電（2330）召開第二季法說會，會前因市場擔憂半導體恐步入下行風險，股價最低來到433元，以年初高點688元計算，波段累積跌幅高達37%，跌勢重於大盤，半導體科技股是這一波大跌的重災區。

‧台積電股價回跌幅度遠高於大盤

法說會上台積電高層釋出樂觀訊息，第二季財報繳出亮眼數字，第二季合併營收5341億元、年增43.5%，毛利率高達59.1%，營業利益率為49.1%，稅後淨利約2370億元，年增76.4%，EPS為9.14元、較去年同期5.18元大幅成長76.4%。獲利表現優於市場原先的預估，最主要理由是受惠產能滿載毛利攀高峰，加上新台幣貶值，挹注收益超越原先財測目標。

　　展望第三季，預估營收將落在198至206億美元之間、季增約9至13%，毛利率落在57.5至59.5%、營益率47至49%。同時亦上調今年美元營收預估值，由先前預期的超過24至29%，上修至成長35%。並看好未來幾年HPC將成為營運主要成長動能，維持未來幾年營收年複合成長率（CAGR）15至20%的長期目標，對長期毛利率達53%以上亦具備信心。

· 台積電今年以來營收維持高成長

年/月	營測收入	月增率	去年同期	年增率	累計營收	年增率
2022/06	175,874,001	-5.29%	148,470,560	18.46%	1,025,216,681	39.57%
2022/05	185,705,425	7.62%	112,359,660	65.20%	849,342,680	44.92%
2022/04	172,561,382	0.35%	111,314,794	55.02%	663,637,255	40.09%
2022/03	171,966,325	17.64%	129,127,886	23.18%	491,075,873	35.50%
2022/02	146,933,238	-14.66%	106,533,690	37.92%	319,109,548	36.79%
2022/01	172,176,110	10.81%	126,749,150	35.84%	172,176,110	35.84%
2021/12	155,382,230	4.90%	117,364,912	32.39%	1,587,415,037	18.53%
2021/11	148,267,599	10.20%	124,865,438	18.74%	1,432,032,807	17.20%

　　在營運利多消息及外資反賣為買的帶動下，台積電股價呈現跌深反彈，**從波段最低433元上漲至505元（7/22）**，只**花了13個交易日**，股價重新站回五百元大關，累積漲幅約

17%，同時也推升指數從低點回升至14996點。

當占大盤權重接近三成的台積電止跌回穩，預期台股再破底的機率相對有限，接下來，只要台積電呈緩步上揚，加上國安基金進場護盤有效提升投資人信心，只要市場的投資信心回升，且目前台股平均本益比僅11倍，以長期投資的角度，我認為現階段是投資人逢低佈局跌深好股票的時機。

以台積電來說，雖然手機、PC、消費性電子需求疲弱，面臨庫存調整是不爭的事實，但在車用、資料中心、HPC需求穩健，公司將產能調配到相關領域，目前產能仍供不應求。

而3奈米與2奈米進度符合預期，3奈米將在今年下半年量產並具備良好良率，在HPC和智慧型手機相關應用的驅動下，2023年將穩定量產，並於2023年上半年開始貢獻營收。

2奈米則預計2024年試產，2025年量產。N2技術將採用奈米片電晶體架構，為客戶提供最好的效能、最佳的成本和技術成熟度，將效能及功耗效率提升一個世代。台積電強調，2奈米製程技術推出時，在密度和能源效率上都將會是業界最先進的技術，將進一步擴展公司的技術領先地位。

原先市場保守預估台積電2022年EPS約落在30元上下，但根據法說會最新財報數據及下半年營運展望，外資上調台積電全年EPS達36元以上，相較於去年23.01元，大幅成長56%！

台積電目前股價約500元，以今年預計EPS達36元計算，本益比還不到14倍，以公司在半導體的領導地位，股價明顯被低估。台積電近五年本益比最高為35倍、最低為14倍，目前本益比落在近五年平均值下緣。

當市場投資的氣氛脫離悲觀時，以台積電的獲利成長性，合理本益比有機會回升至20倍以上（近五年平均本益比約落在25倍），假設市場給予台積電20倍本益比，則合理股價會來到720元，只要台積電營運展望維持公司高層的預估，股價應該還有很高的潛在上漲空間。

除了台積電外，**如果你擔憂電子股的股價起伏過大，我認為持有較不受景氣影響的民生消費股，也是現階段納入投資組合的好選擇之一**，比方像是平價連鎖餐飲－八方雲集（2753）、超商龍頭－統一超（2912）、包材飲料代工大廠－宏全（9939）等，今年以來不受股市大跌影響，皆繳出8~19%的正報酬率。

以宏全來說，公司過去20年不曾出現虧損，近13年每年EPS皆在3元以上，現金股利配發皆在2元以上，生產的主要產品雖然是不起眼的寶特瓶，但近幾年的獲利卻能持續成長，顯示公司在經營上確實有值得我們深入研究的獨到之處。

宏全為台灣最具規模的飲料瓶蓋、寶特瓶飲料生產商，主要客戶包含統一、可口可樂、百事可樂、黑松、愛之味、泰山、康師傅等，產品主要包括四大類，分別為飲料代工、瓶蓋及瓶身製品、標籤及薄膜製品、電子及機械類製品。從個別項目銷售到組合式合併銷售，再到組裝全配套銷售，提供客戶一貫化服務。

生產基地遍布台灣、中國、東南亞與非洲，全球共擁有48座生產基地，其中駐點於客戶工廠的生產基地約21座（In House廠中廠）。近年開始佈局東南亞、非洲市場發展，除了代工之外，宏全在東南亞也首次進入自有品牌飲料經營。

・宏全2020至今2022年週線走勢圖

　　我在多年前就有留意到宏全的營運表現頗為穩定，不過獲利僅維持平穩，並非我心目中的成長股，雖然殖利率都維持在5%以上，但充其量只能算是一檔價值股。

　　2013年統一集團將訂單轉移到自家旗下的統一實（9907），造成原本佔宏全中國業績50%的訂單，在兩年後僅剩3%，是公司獲利連續好幾年無法成長的重要原因。但宏全積極開發新客戶，加上積極拓展東南亞市場，EPS從2018年開始連續三年正成長，2021年EPS達6.83元，創上市新高紀錄。

　　展望2022年，第一季合併營收56.1億元、年增9.5%，在匯兌收益使得業外高於原先預期下，稅後淨利5.55億、年增15.6%，EPS達1.93元，表現優於市場預期。 法人預估全年三大主力營運地區中，東南亞將成為成長最大引擎，營收年增15~20%，其次為中國年增約10~15%、台灣則約為5~10%。

　　東南亞地區則是今年重中之重，尤其人口數最多的印尼更是宏全在東協發展的重點市場，印尼Sosro及泗水第二條

產線已分別於2021年5月及11月投產後，今年初生產效率已達八成，今年貢獻度持續加溫；至於菲律賓則延後到今年建廠，預估在新產線加入投產後，可望挹注更多動能。

宏全的競爭優勢在於不斷創新自身的商業模式，掌握市場發展趨勢與客戶需求，繼2000年提供瓶蓋、標籤、PET瓶組合式銷售、2003年上市後，再擴充飲料代工填充業務，到成為代工代料、ODM、駐廠連線服務、合作合資的製造業服務化。獨創的IN-HOUSE模式，由瓶蓋、瓶胚、吹瓶設備、至飲料充填，提供客戶一條龍全方位垂直整合服務。

宏全目前本益比僅10倍左右，加上長期殖利高達5%以上，在經濟前景仍不明朗的此刻，具備穩健獲利且高配息的宏全，是現階段攻守兼備的好選擇。

・在獲利提升下宏全現金股利亦逐年成長

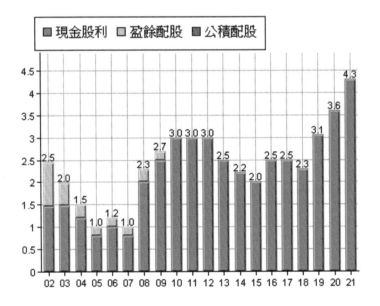

在股票市場上遵循八二法則，兩成不到的人賺錢，而這些人取得市場超過八成獲利。但不幸的是，我們可能都花超過八成的時間，來分析總體經濟與預期股市走勢這種對我們的投資獲利只有兩成貢獻的事情。

把時間拉長，投資人的報酬率與公司長期獲利表現息息相關，而本波段股市大幅回檔修正，也讓很多好公司的股價跌落至合理、甚至低估價，沒有人能夠確切知道大盤後續的走勢，但我知道，從長線的角度來看，這裡肯定是買點而非賣點，不管是台積電或是台股。

※本篇分析為個人意見，僅供參考。

【重點整理】

★台積電財報第二季成績亮眼，上調今年美元營收預估值。股價跌深反彈，從波段最低的433漲回500，只花了13個交易日。

★當占了大盤權重近三成的台積電止跌回穩，台股再破底的機率相對有限。

★擔憂電子股起伏太大，可選擇較不受景氣影響的民生消費股。

★平價餐飲、超商龍頭、包材飲料代工大廠…等，觀察公司是否因應局勢，創新自身的商業模式，並掌握市場趨勢和消費者需求。

★許多好公司在這波跌幅中跌到合理、甚至低估價，出手之前務必做好健全的評估。

做好面臨風險的準備，妥善分配資金部位

張皓傑

後疫情時代，升息救通膨是必要措施

今年股市流年不利，諸多因素導致全球股市同步下跌委靡不振，投資人人心惶惶。2022年1月5日台股迎來了歷史新高點18620點，卻又一路跌跌撞撞，至7/12最低點來到13928點，跌幅達-25.2%，究竟最近市場出了什麼問題？

自2021年疫情持續蔓延，全球航運大亂，運費飆漲，各產業缺工導致工資上漲，以及各地封城影響全球供應鏈，供給面出了狀況、貨出不來，而需求卻不減反增，再加上先前因為疫情，各國祭出寬鬆貨幣政策試圖刺激經濟，及年初烏俄開戰惡化了能源供給面，種種因素疊加之下，供需出現了嚴重失衡，最終導致美國面臨了40年來最嚴重的通貨膨脹。

若這樣的通膨持續惡化，恐導致你我手上的貨幣實質購買力大幅萎縮，更嚴重可能導致鈔票變成廢紙，不可不慎。燃眉之急之下，美國不得不陸續升息，目的就是收回市場上的資金，先減緩大家的消費力道，需求減弱後，供給得以慢慢消化，進而使物價穩定，目標要讓通膨率回到2%正常水準。**以政策面來說，升息非常正當也有其必要性，只要投資**

人能理解來龍去脈，其實升息並不是什麼壞事。

升息政策後，使得資金從各國股匯市退出，回流美國，導致股匯市雙殺，這是升息帶來的不利因素。台股歷經2020和2021年的暴漲以後，也應適時的做調節，如同鐘擺般來回擺盪，這將有助於後市重整完畢再度上攻。

參考過去股市大幅下跌的經驗，避免恐慌心態

在這個階段，投資人最關心的事，莫過於下跌會跌到哪裡？以及會跌多久？我們不妨借鏡台股過去的歷史經驗，來判讀未來可能的走向。下表我整理過去（包含今年）台股歷經較大跌幅的四次事件，第一次是1990年的證交稅實施後，最大跌幅達到-80.4%，總共歷時242天（為計算上方便，此天數包含例假日），第二次為2000年網路泡沫，跌幅為-67.18%，總共歷時586天，第三次則為2007年次級房貸，跌幅為-59.88%，歷時388天。

從前三次事件來看，好消息是，可以看出跌幅一次比一次小，這歸因於現代健全的金融體制，及政府良好的政策管控，因此就算今年最大的跌幅已達-25.2%，我仍保持正向看待，下跌最終仍有一定的底線，不要無限上綱帶給自己不必要的恐慌。

另外，三次事件中最長歷時586天，大約是一年半的時間，也可以此作為下跌天數的最大值，投資人只要過一年半，應該就有很大的機會度過下跌危機。

從18620（2022/01/05）點起計算至2022/07/12最低點，已歷時188天，若以前三次的歷時平均數405天來算的話，約

下跌到2023/02/14可以見到曙光，若以最長天數586天推算的話，則會到2023/08/14抵達終點。雖然這些都是用歷史看未來的估算值，不見得準確，但仍可以讓我們心中有一個底，了解下跌終究會結束。

· 台股歷來遇重大事件之震盪表現

年份/事件	最高	最低	跌幅	歷時（天）
1990 年證交稅實施	12682	2485	-80.40%	242
2000 年網路泡沫化	10394	3412	-67.18%	586
2007 年次級房貸	9860	3955	-59.88%	388
2022 烏俄戰、美國升息	18620	13928	-25.20%	188

資料來源：加權股價指數維基百科，期間：1990~2022年。

面對下跌時，應該做的四個準備

無論你是什麼投資門派，技術面投資、價值面投資抑或是籌碼面投資，保持正確的投資心態，是能在股海中長期屹立不搖的關鍵。而面對下跌，我們要如何保持平常心，並樂觀看待，以下分享幾點我的看法。

（1）投資前務必了解投資風險

大家在面對投資想的都是「賺錢」二字，其實更首要的思考應該要聚焦在「風險」，沒有風險管理的概念，就先別想著獲利。當你投入一筆資金，請先思考這筆資金的投資風險在哪裡，這筆資金有可能賠多少？最壞的狀況是什麼？我可以承擔這樣的投資虧損嗎？資產的每日波動是我可以承受的嗎？這筆資金三年以內我有可能用到嗎？一旦想清楚上述問題，你才能夠進一步想，有可能獲利多少。

投資能帶來獲利，正因為冒著「可以承受的風險」，投資如果沒有任何風險，那就會像定存一樣，只能帶來少少的獲利。你會知道「下跌」對股市而言應該是非常稀鬆平常的狀況，是因為早已經事先沙盤推演過，這些都應該是你心裡預期會有的狀況，當真正發生了，就可以平常心面對。

（2）找尋絕佳投資機會

從歷史數據來看，上漲的天數比下跌的天數還多，一年大跌的次數只有一、兩次，通常這時候就是投資的絕佳時機，記得在這個時候想想看，有哪些你平常覺得股價硬梆梆，想買卻又覺得貴鬆鬆的優質好公司，在下跌的時候就是你把握機會的好時刻，想像股市在做一年一次的週年慶大拍賣，不趁這時候撿便宜，難道要等到股價漲高高再來追高嗎？

（3）妥善規劃資金運用

千萬要記住，現金是你的彈藥庫，很多人往往在大跌的前幾天，就把彈藥庫給用光了，這時候只能看著股價持續下跌，卻又愛莫能助。切記要做好規劃，把資金切成至少五等分或十等分，並且預先設定好的進場價位，分批進場，降低投資成本，尤其現在有了盤中零股交易，應多加善加利用，有時候小額資金進場，靈活度會更高，不會在一個價位就卡了大筆資金。

（4）忽略市場各種煽動人心的雜音

許多人當市場下跌，由於內心的慌張，便亟欲想要找到安定內心的避風港，這時候便喜歡上論壇看網友的討論，或

是過度關心報章雜誌媒體，其實這些都是沒有必要的事情，看太多反而自亂陣腳，各種煽動人心的言論更是對穩定軍心沒有幫助，由於群眾效應，這時候往往會「造成投資人過度恐慌的心理」。其實只要確切了解下跌的原因，並知道市場的表現會如鐘擺般在漲跌之間來回擺盪，且長期來看仍會向上攻破前次高點（人類發展持續進步及穩定的通膨），那麼其他的資訊便不看也罷。

下跌防禦的投資三妙招

投資人面對下跌，絕對不能坐以待斃，事先防範是非常重要的，幫你的資產預先做好防禦，就像提前做好防颱準備一樣，一旦做足了準備，真正強颱來襲，也能在家中平安度過，待颱風過去以後，仍是雨過天晴，風和日麗。

如何幫自己的資產做好防禦，分享給投資人三個投資妙招：

（1）保持正確的投資心態

誰都想買在起漲點、賣在起跌點，但在實務上，擇時進出的難度非常高，以機率來說就像中樂透，就算讓你猜中一次，只要資金持續曝險在市場，仍要面對下一次的漲跌，如果沒有正確的投資心態，還是無法在股海中穩定向前行。

面對下跌，應以不變應萬變，除了要注意不要將未來五年有可能會用到的資金投入股市，最好的投資方式就是，以定期定額累積資產，下跌可以享受買便宜，上漲更可以享受資產的增值，更可以免除下單時內心的掙扎。

（2）做好資產配置分散投資

從這次台股下跌集中在電子類股來看，若是投資人集中單一持股，下跌時受到的損害是相當大的。最好的做法應是做好資產配置，分散投資在不同產業類別及債券，才能降低風險。而透過ETF投資，其實就能簡單達到資產配置的效益。

（3）口袋中股息型ETF不可少

股息型ETF持有配息率較高的股票，這些高股息的標的，平常的股價波動也相較來得平穩，一旦遇到市場波動下跌，往往下跌的幅度也是最小，具有穩定軍心的效果，可以讓晚上睡得更安穩。而更大的好處是，當遇到下跌迫使資金卡住時，較高的股息配發率可以讓現金流保有一定的水平，股息可以緩解現金水位的枯竭，除了因應生活所需，還可作為下跌加碼的利器。

下表為幾支股息型ETF，元大台灣高股息低波動ETF（00713）及國泰台灣ESG永續高股息ETF（00878）自今年以來的報酬，分別為-6.66%及-10.36%。以台股為投資範疇的一般型ETF共有29檔（不含槓桿型及反向型），這兩檔分別排名位居第三名跟第五名，表現位於ETF當中的前段班。相較於代表大盤的發行量加權股價報酬指數下跌-17.34%，以及富邦台灣50ETF的-19.03%，股息型ETF下跌幅度相較小，顯示其下跌的防禦能力是相當不錯的。

· 選擇跌幅小的高股息ETF組合，把損失降到最低

(數據截至 111/06/30)	自今年以來報酬	自今年以來報酬排名
元大台灣高股息低波動ETF	-6.66%	3 / 29
國泰台灣ESG永續高股息ETF	-10.36%	5 / 29
發行量加權股價報酬指數	-17.34%	-
富邦台灣采吉50ETF	-19.03%	14 / 29

資料來源：投信投顧公會基金績效評比及台灣證券交易所，
期間：2022/01/03~06/30。

※本篇分析為個人意見，僅供參考。

【重點整理】

★通膨若繼續惡化，紙幣可能變廢紙！升息非常正當，也有
  其必要，了解背後原因就能理解並非壞事。

★參考過去下跌的經驗，包含跌幅和歷經天數，估算這次的
  下跌底線，不用無限上綱、過度恐慌。

★「跌」和「漲」都是股市的正常運作，趁跌的時候妥善規
  劃資金部位，尋找優質但平時難以入手的公司，想像成
  「週年慶」檔期在折扣。

★股息型ETF平時的股價波動相較之下平穩，遇到市場波動
  時，受到影響也最小，晚上可以睡得安穩一些。

★較高的股息配發率，可以讓現金流保持一定水平，做為下
  跌加碼的利器。

〈後疫情時代的股市趨勢分析和投資建議〉（3）

對抗通膨和不穩定的時代，找到穩定的核心資產項目

葉芷娟

　　朋友間今年常互相調侃：「2021年感覺股票怎麼都不會跌，2022年感覺股票怎麼都不會漲，好兩極呀！」只能說今年真的是很特別，疫情、通膨、升息、縮表、戰爭全都加在一起，過去單一利空因素股市就會震盪了，何況這次一口氣全都來。

　　如果用數據來說話，統計金融海嘯後幾次美股修正，修正幅度不是重點，重點是「修正時間」，過去7次修正，平均90天就會結束，短則13天就會反彈，然而今年這波回檔一回就回了161天，是近來最久的一次，修正跌幅也大於過去平均，怪不得讓大家好有感！

金融危機後，美股S&P500修正情況		
修正起訖日	修正跌幅(%)	修正長度(天)
2010/4/23 - 2010/7/2　歐債問題	-16.0	70
2011/4/29 - 2011/10/3　歐債危機及美債降評	-19.4	157
2015/5/21 - 2015/8/25　新興國家經濟轉弱	-12.4	96
2015/11/3 - 2016/2/11　FED開始升息	-13.3	100
2018/1/26 - 2018/2/8　貿易戰	-10.2	13
2018/9/20 - 2018/12/24　縮表及經濟動能轉弱	-19.8	95
2020/2/19 - 2020/3/23　新冠肺炎疫情	-33.9	33
2022/1/3 - 2022/6/13　FED加速升息及將縮表	-21.8	161
平均值	-18.4	90.6

股災教會我的事：熊出沒！債券也會跌

過去傳統投資學都教我們：當有風險出現時，可以找避險資產躲一下。所謂避險資產，不外乎黃金、債券。但幾次股災中，我發現這些避險資產其實一點也不避險，常和股票一樣說跌就跌。

我歸納出的結論是：**在非戰爭造成的系統性風險中，一旦波動過大，所有的避險商品都會跟著暫時失效**。因為以黃金來說，實務上鮮少人會真的拿現金去買金條回來放在家裡，大部分人都是透過金融衍生性商品來買黃金，既然是金融衍生商品，就有槓桿成分在裡面，所以當股市重挫、市場風險波動過大時，大家會「去槓桿」，把黃金賣掉、把債券賣掉，畢竟「現金為王」，這時候真正最抗跌的只有「美元現金」，若真要操作避險資產，反而「美元指數」才是真正能操作的避險工具。

股災教會我的事：停損要快、狠、準

每當遇上統性風險時，短期投機的持股，停損一定要快、狠、準。投資市場裡有這樣的說法：「做多賺得多，做空賺得快！」想要賺20%一個波段可能要花至少一季左右的時間，但股災來臨時，可能三、五天就跌20%了。

因此，苗頭不對，忍痛停損賣出一定要快，千萬不要以為沒關係給它跌，擺著等回升就好。大家要知道100元股票跌到80元，是跌20%，但要漲回到100元，不是20%，是要漲25%；100元股票跌到70元，是跌30%，但要漲回100元，可是要漲43%，真的不容易。

抗通膨投資術：轉嫁成本給消費者的能力

如今的時空背景，我們既要面對20年來最大的電子庫存修正期，還要對抗40年來最強的通貨膨脹，投資選股要能「抗波動」更要能「抗通膨」。我覺得這時投資有3大重點：**（1）轉嫁通膨成本給消費者的能力，（2）高殖利率股，（3）股價位階不能太高。**

台股裡誰最有轉嫁通膨成本給消費者的能力？絕對是「食品股」。畢竟大家手機可以多用幾年、電視可以多看幾年，但不能不吃飯啊！因此，1210大成，兩岸最大的白肉雞電宰加工廠，事業涵蓋各種飼料、鮮肉食品及加工品，其中肉品主要供應給好市多、肯德基、麥當勞、21世紀風味館等通路，占整體營收超過2成比重。1215卜蜂，農畜肉、肉類加工品占整體營收6成。全台灣最大的食品廠1216統一，民生必需食品起家，公司營收乳品占3成、飼料2成7、泡麵1成1。尤其這類食品股利向來都不差，當央行政策利率上升之際，高殖利率也更護體。

再來，能轉嫁通膨成本的還有「基礎建設股」，也就是所謂和政府做生意的公司。在國外，政府會把港口、機場、鐵路甚至高速公路都以特許經營的方式，交由民間企業來運營，而為了確保公司利益，這些公司都會跟政府簽訂轉嫁成本的條款。例如：運營澳洲、加拿大和美國多條高速公路的Transurban，就和政府明文約定，通行費可每季隨通膨調整，直接把通膨轉嫁給消費者。這類公司也是抗通膨投資裡很好的標的，可惜台灣比較沒有。

不過，同樣會被劃進和政府做生意基礎建設相關範疇

的，還有由政策主導推動的產業，目前擁有最大商機的就屬「綠能產業」。雖然講到綠能大家會直覺聯想到乾淨能源的太陽能發電，但太陽能並非高技術門檻的產業，紅色供應鏈大舉來襲，毛利起不來，而且台灣的太陽能類股多半只供應國內市場，較難吃到全球綠能基礎建設商機。

相形之下，「充電樁」就是電動車順暢上路最重要的關鍵基礎建設，世界各國的電動車充電樁遠遠跟不上電動車銷售數量，2020年美國的車樁比為16：1，歐盟10：1，最積極的中國也不過6：1，都離2：1標準還有很大的距離。

目前國內充電樁相關個股，最具代表性的非2308台達電莫屬，台達電在這領域已經深耕多年，在慢充和快充系統，交流充電樁和直流充電樁的規格都非常齊全，充電樁也已獲得BMW、特斯拉、泰國三菱汽車、菲律賓捷豹路虎等車廠採用，公司也曾表示未來充電樁業務都會有五成以上的速度成長，成為公司營收獲利的一大來源。

另外，充電樁中的充電槍，3023信邦已通過美國、中國和歐洲的認證，而且為充電樁營運龍頭ChargePoint充電槍槍頭和線束供應商。也為中國豪華電動車品牌蔚來汽車提供充電槍、家用充電線束，今年蔚來將發布三款新車，也將會是信邦重要的成長動能。

烏俄戰爭下的思考：台灣的隱形軍工股工業電腦

最後想談談烏俄戰爭，我認為這場戰役會讓全世界各國都重新開始思考自己的軍事戰力到底夠不夠？同時提高戰備支出。美國的雷神和洛克希德馬丁是典型軍工受惠概念股，

但台灣沒有直接供應的概念股。台股軍工概念股直覺會想到2634漢翔、2208台船、8383千附，但這些充其量也只是台灣國防自主概念股罷了，跟世界各國增加武器支出不一樣。

台灣的隱形軍工類股其實是「工業電腦」，而這也是台灣最能沾到各國戰備支出的領域，畢竟現在戰爭已是電子化的科技戰，軍用的筆電、軍用的平板都是戰爭裡的隱形角色，2395研華、6166凌華、3005神基、6414樺漢、4916事欣科，都已佈局軍工規產品許多年。

股市操作，核心資產、衛星持股分清楚

本書作者遠藤洋在書中提到：股票投資的基本就是「找出」有希望的個股，「買進」和「賣出」這三個步驟。看似簡單，但要如何找、如何買、如何賣，箇中高手都有各自心法。

以我自己來說，我的股票分為核心資產部位，原則上買進後就鮮少賣出，主要目的以每年領股息為主，採左側交易。人不投機杆少年，另一部分專門做價差的衛星持股部位，我會搭著市場熱度話題右側交易追趨勢買進，但嚴守停利、停損原則，賺波段快錢。二種完全不同交易模式的投資，我直接分成二個證券帳戶操作，切換不同的證券帳戶APP時，腦子也較能跟著轉換。

不管如何最重要的是要有明確的投資戰略，相信大家都能找到優游於股海中的樂趣。

※本篇分析為個人意見，僅供參考。

【重點整理】

★當熊市出現，黃金、債券等避險資產，一樣會跌！現金為
　王，美元指數做為避險的工具較為實際。

★對抗通膨，尋找「可以轉嫁成本給消費者」的公司，例如
　食品股和政策主導推進的產業。

★目前政府推動的綠能產業，比起太陽能相關企業，不如看
　看電動車必備的「充電樁」。

★在烏俄戰爭後，全球各國都會思考自己的軍事戰力。台灣
　投資人則可注意隱形軍工類股：工業電腦。

★想要降低風險、又想做些價差？用兩種交易APP，一個是
　長期的核心資產，另一個操作熱門話題、有市場熱度的衛
　星股，並嚴守停利停損原則。

〈後疫情時代的股市趨勢分析和投資建議〉（4）

健全投資心態：以成長優先，把握低檔時機！

股海老牛

2020年由於新冠疫情在全球出現大流行，受到恐慌情緒影響，全球金融市場價格急遽下跌，美股更是出現了4次熔斷（在股市交易時間內，當價格波動幅度達到某個限度，就會暫停交易一段時間）。美國為了挽救經濟，宣佈實行量化寬鬆政策（QE），當股市注入QE的資金猛藥，使得全球股市瞬間進入Ｖ型反轉。「最壞的時代，卻迎來最好的一年」，不少年輕人看上股市大幅修正，而勇於錢進股市，以至於近幾年開戶人數高達百萬以上。在股市屢創新高下，甚至在餐廳吃飯、坐電梯時，都能聽到隔壁在談論熱門的股票。

反觀今年進入縮表升息，並且受到俄烏戰爭影響，全球進入通膨緊縮的情況，再加上FED頻頻發出經濟衰退的警訊，導致股市也從高點回落超過20%以上，正式邁入熊市。而台灣今年6月景氣對策信號綜合判斷分數為27分，燈號連續4個月出現綠燈，顯示今年景氣放緩，並且保守看待未來景氣。

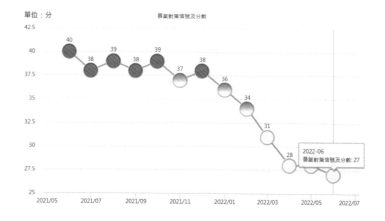

單位：分

景氣對策信號及分數

2022-06
景氣對策信號及分數: 27

　　「覆巢之下無完卵」，在面臨空頭修正時期，即使是財報好獲利佳的績優股仍無法倖免；在股價連續下跌時，也就是說若是今年買進的朋友，帳上應該多為損失。悲觀的人看到帳面數字，就忘記怎麼笑了；而樂觀的人反而能從容不迫，從中看到遍地黃金的時機到了，股價回落就是難得的佈局良機。同一件事可以有不同態度檢視，只是我們的「底氣」夠不夠足而已！

靠運氣贏來的，憑實力輸回去！

　　對投資新手來說，今年的兩大考驗：

☑ 空頭走勢，勿輕易接刀

　　在資金狂潮的推動之下，台股在2020及2021年分別上漲2735點及3486點。大家也習慣下跌再加碼的節奏，**但當進入空頭時，當你還是習慣越跌越買的話，就如同下跌的刀一般，接到滿手血。**老牛的建議是，一定要等到逐步止跌回穩後，再逢低買進即可。

☑ 震盪波動愈來愈大

　　這幾年由於大筆資金錢進股市，再加上當沖客的盛行，不只是個股出現漲跌的幅度加大，甚至指數也有波動度越來越大的情況。譬如今年6月就出現單月下跌近2千點，幅度也近-12%，這是以前少見的情況。這也表示「非理性下跌」狀況，即使金管會出來信心喊話，仍無法見效。

　　所以對於剛踏入股市的朋友，最大的問題就是「憑感覺」操作；在尚未建立正確的投資心態時，心中應該都會經歷過一段天使與惡魔的交戰過程；而且每個階段的疑慮各都不同，當下看起來很合理，但事後都發現非常離譜。

調整投資節奏

　　老牛所推行的「抱緊處理」四大心法，是從過去閱讀大量的投資理財書籍、股市交易經驗中，所孕育出來的。每個字都屬獲利關鍵、缺一不可：

　　「抱」：挑到好公司就要一直抱著。

　　「緊」：以好價格買進才抱得緊。

　　「處」：上下震盪能處變不驚，不敗在情緒。

　　「理」：理智配置投資組合，順勢加減碼。

　　然而，譬如今年位於空頭期間，「處」變不驚則顯得特別重要，尤其股價上下震盪劇烈，不少人經不起股市下跌、看到帳上虧損而心煩難耐，結果隨意變賣手中績優股，之後等到整體股市反彈回穩，也買不回當初的低價格，只能眼睜睜看著績優股的魚尾被別人整碗抱走，那不是很可惜嗎？趁著下跌空頭時，重新調整投資心態才是最重要的。就像馬拉

松的跑者般，別被外界的殺聲隆隆影響，以中長期投資的步伐前進，調整好自己的投資節奏。

黑夜離去，迎來曙光

碰上去年的需求高基期，今年可預見的是終端消費產業（筆電、手機、面板）碰上砍單出現衰退疑慮。不少半導體產業鏈大廠也出現雜音，陸續發出庫存量上升的警訊，據傳需要約半年的時間，才能完成庫存調整。再碰上升息年，不只是對股市有影響，當然也會衝擊到房市；雖不能完全抑制房價上漲，但我們可以發現到新屋銷售的確相對降溫不少。

今年的空方消息確實較以往複雜並且同時發生，從年初的俄烏戰爭、油價瘋漲、再到通膨升息等等變數，就連獲利成長、基本面穩健的公司，都不敵籌碼大舉抽離的影響。這時大多數投資人操作心態都會偏向保守或止損，藉以避開股災帶來的恐懼，但就是以「**投資情緒**」也間接主導操作判斷，長期來看往往都是過於保守而卻錯過大賺的機會。從股市漲跌循環圖中，老牛認為在空頭急跌修正後，在經過低檔整理之後，終將重回緩步回升的軌道上。

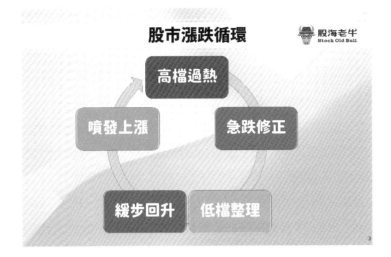

股市漲跌循環　股海老牛 Stock Old Bull

成長優先，把握低檔

　　從產業的大方向來看，**老牛認為電動車／網通／半導體仍是未來3-5年的趨勢**，從該產業中分別挑出兩家過去獲利表現優秀的個股，作為深入說明的案例。分別為電動車：宇隆（2233）、建和興（3033）；網通：智易（3596）、智邦（2345）；半導體：帆宣（6196）、崇越（5434）。

　　從2021年的績優表現到2022年的獲利分析來切入，說明挑選個股的重點。尤其是在產業發展的大方向下，乘著成長的順風前進，才能在股市中獲利成長安心抱緊。

・個股營收及獲利表現

類股	代號	名稱	股價（元）	本益比	上半年營收年增率（％）	第一季EPS（元）
電動車	2233	宇隆	116	11.8	5.07	3
	3003	健和興	83.2	15.5	9.85	1.59
網通	3596	智易	120	15.1	10.5	1.8
	2345	智邦	248	28.4	26.3	2.31
半導體	6196	帆宣	110	12.5	47.4	1.89
	5434	崇越	153.5	11.2	29.6	3.63

製表：股海老牛，資料日期：2022/7/28

📌 宇隆（2233）

宇隆是一家精密金屬零件製造商。宇隆的產品結構大多為車用相關。受惠目前全球排碳趨勢，電車概念已成為顯學，宇隆也能無縫接軌將原有的零件製程轉型至電車領域。

由於過去的獲利表現優秀，今年被縫紉機製造大廠伸興（1558）進行股權收購，等同是多角化投資。老牛過去就認為投資一家持續獲利的公司，除了可以降低倒閉的風險，也可以提高被溢價收購的機率，這是老牛認為投資好公司的重要性。

📌 健和興（3003）

建和興成立44年，上市至今已20年。其主要業務為端子、光源系統零組件、電子連接器等。產品應用極為廣泛，其中電工／綠能連接器佔比較多，2013年跨入汽車應用，同時供應電動車充電連接器，成功打入電動車「充電槍」題材。車用佔比逐年成長，搭上近期最夯的電動車題材。

📌 智易（3596）

智易是專業網通產品代工廠，營運模式採直接出貨給客戶，因此毛利率較一般代工廠高。且客戶主要以電信商為主，零售通路產品佔比較低。智易目前歐洲、美國客戶營收合計高達8成；隨著疫情趨緩，再加上固網寬頻產品升級，也有利於智易產品平均價格提升。

📌 智邦（2345）

網通業在2021年碰上缺料危機，即使是訂單滿檔卻是出不貨的無奈；今年隨著料況緩解，帶動業績大爆發。一樣受惠於固網頻寬升級帶動換機潮，以及影音串流需求增長，並且未來有雲端籍資料中心等訂單挹注，獲利有望同步成長。

📌 帆宣（6196）

帆宣提供無塵室系統工程、氣體供應系統等服務，也是全球最大半導體顯影設備商艾司摩爾（ASML）的系統模組代工廠。受惠於半導體擴廠，增加資本支出，帆宣就是受惠廠商；目前在手訂單突破600億元，隨著建廠進度進入認列高峰期，營收及獲利也同樣能維持在高檔水準。

📌 崇越（5434）

崇越近年在半導體擴廠題材的加持下，獲利穩定成長，主要代理銷售半導體、光電、電子材料各類產品，提供整合服務，並從事環保及廠務系統處理工程。

其中，半導體材料占產品營收八成（包括光阻液、研磨液、矽晶圓、石英材料、晶圓載具為主），位於半導體產業的中游位置。下游合作廠商多為半導體知名大廠，除長期供

應台積電相關製程材料為最大宗外，其餘客戶則為大陸中芯國際、聯電、華亞科、南亞科、世界先進等。

· 個股2021年營運表現

類股	代號	名稱	2021年營收（億）	2021年營收成長率（%）	2021年毛利率（%）	2021年EPS（元）	2021年盈餘成長率（%）	2021年ROE（%）
電動車	2233	宇隆	32.3	27.4	35.6	9.01	44.6	17.7
	3003	健和興	47.9	41.7	35.5	4.98	115	15.1
網通	3596	智易	382	13.3	13.9	8.6	2.87	13.7
	2345	智邦	596	9.43	19	8.44	-6.95	31.3
半導體	6196	帆宣	345	37.2	10.5	8.24	68.9	21.3
	5434	崇越	427	18	12.2	12.63	11	20.5

製表：股海老牛

　　最後，能在股市中真正累積財富的人，幾乎都是採取價值型投資，讓資產像雪球般越滾越大，總能克服心理因素來判別進出場依據。就像股神巴菲特最近在股東會上表示近期將大買特買，別人的恐懼又成為他貪婪的泉源。

　　營運良好的公司不會被疫情打垮、不會被金融風暴擊倒、更不會被升息給拖累，反而能在這一次次的挑戰中越發成長、更加茁壯，所以我希望大家，一定要記住「價值投資」這項投資必勝準則。

※本篇分析為個人意見，僅供參考。

★把握低檔和空頭走勢，但千萬別亂接刀！逢低買進有個前提，那就是等止跌回升的時候，不要越跌越買，還說服自己在撿便宜。

★烏俄戰爭、油價飆漲、通膨升息……，今年空方消息不僅複雜且同時發生，把握股價「低檔整理期」，以成長股為優先挑選對象。

★從產業大方向評估，電動車、網通和半導體，仍然會是未來至少三~五年的趨勢！乘著「成長」的順風前進，才能在股市中獲利、安心抱緊。

★營運良好的公司，在今年也難敵多重發生的空方消息，但絕對不會被擊垮，反而會更加成長茁壯。

審慎規劃，做足功課，才是正確的投資心態。

以上分析和建議為個人意見，理性評估公司基本面，認知投資一定有風險，訂出可接受的損益點，不做自己心理無法承受的投資。希望各位讀者都能找到適合自己的投資步調。

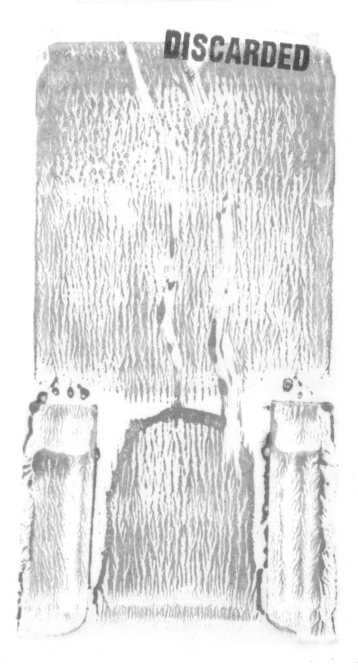

Library of Contemporary Architects

SKIDMORE, OWINGS & MERRILL

Library of Contemporary Architects

SKIDMORE, OWINGS & MERRILL

Introduction and notes by
CHRISTOPHER WOODWARD

with 73 photographs by
YUKIO FUTAGAWA

SIMON AND SCHUSTER NEW YORK

Copyright © 1970 by Thames and Hudson Ltd, London
Photographs copyright © 1968 by Yukio Futagawa

Published in the United States by Simon and Schuster
Rockefeller Center, 630 Fifth Avenue
New York, New York 10020

First U.S. printing

First published in Japan in 1968 by Bijutsu Shuppan-sha, Tokyo, in their series
GENDAI KENCHIKUKA SHIRIZU.
New texts have been provided for this English language edition.

SBN 671-20696-6
Library of Congress Catalog Card Number: 79-120905

Printed in Japan

Contents

Introduction

'GENERAL STATEMENT

The firm of Skidmore, Owings & Merrill was founded in 1936. Nineteen General Partners direct the work in four principal offices—New York, Chicago, San Francisco and Portland, Oregon. A staff of approximately 1,000 architects, engineers and technicians enables the firm to furnish complete services in the fields/of planning, designing, engineering and supervising construction of building projects. . .

Each project, depending on its scale and type, requires integration of the following services in varying combinations to best meet the client's needs:

Programming and Site Selection
Architectural Planning and Design
Preparation of Working Drawings and Specifications
Engineering Design (Structural, Mechanical and Civil)
Master and Site Planning
Site Engineering and Landscape Design
Preparation of Reports
Preparation of Cost Estimates and Appraisals
Preparation of Bills of Materials and Requisitions
Field Inspection and Supervision of Construction
Management and Co-ordination of Large-scale Projects'

From *SOM Handbook*, November 1968

It is now almost as difficult to *see* Lever House nearly twenty years after its completion as it is to recognize palazzi of the Renaissance in Florence from the engravings of their elevations. But in 1952, the building whose model had formed the climax of the Museum of Modern Art's 1950 exhibition of SOM's work stood shining unprecedentedly, its podium clad in stainless steel, nudging McKim, Meade and White's Racquet club to the south. Today, since Seagram[1] was built diagonally opposite —itself now flanked by broken-up Lever imitations—Lever House is disappearing like Alberti's Palazzo Rucellai.

The partnership between Louis Skidmore (1897–1962) and Nathaniel Owings (b. 1903) was formed in 1936 after both had worked on designs for the 'Century of Progress' Exposition at Chicago in 1933. In 1937 Gordon Bunshaft (born at Buffalo, N.Y., 1909) joined the New York office which Skidmore had just set up, Owings continuing to keep a small office in Chicago. Bunshaft had trained at Massachusetts Institute of Technology at a time when the effects of ten years of Corbusian Heroic propaganda—from *Vers une Architecture* (1923) to the Villa Savoie (1931)—were eroding the Beaux-Arts syllabus, and on leaving MIT he toured in Europe and North Africa on a travelling fellowship until 1937. John Merrill (b. 1896) joined the firm in 1939. Bunshaft became a full partner of the firm, together with William Brown, Robert Cutler and J. Walter Severinghaus in 1946.

The firm expanded, finally up to 450, and set up a special office to deal with its largest operation during the war: the design of 'Atom City', Oak Ridge, Tennessee, a new town serving the Manhattan project, whose population grew from nothing in 1942 to 75,000 by 1946, built at an eventual cost of 120 million dollars. The town's requirements for isolation, and vast amounts of electricity which could be supplied by the Tennessee Valley Authority, led to its location on mile-wide Oak Ridge. The expanding plan, finally extending six miles along the ridge, disposed 15,000 family houses, the first 3,000 in prefabricated asbestos-cement board panels, 13,000 dormitory units, 5,000 trailers and 16,000 hutments and barracks, along gently meandering tracks. Except for the absence of the grid-iron plan, it is pure American frontier. The same ordinary Americanness is evident in two other wartime designs: the little shopping centre at Aero Acres, Middle River, Maryland, a 2,000 family development by Martin Corporation, which recreates a western

11

Main Street, but with vehicular servicing at the back and parking meters instead of hitching posts at the front; and the Breueresque recreation buildings at Great Lakes Naval Training Center, 1942.

Chicago Land Commission provided SOM's office there with their first large job after the war: clearance of a vast area of South Side slums, and a 20 million dollar investment by an insurance company to house 1,400 families.[2] The first published Lake Meadows project, had it been built and were it not for the creepy social engineering involved, would have eclipsed the achievement of the later housing at Park Hill, Sheffield, England (built 1955–61). It posited two vast buildings, 23 storeys high, 832 feet long and one apartment (40 feet) deep, running east-west between South Parkway and the lakeside railroad. The buildings were separated from each other by a landscaped park, with a suburban-style shopping centre to the south, and some row houses were to be set between the blocks looking over the railroad to the lake. *Architectural Forum* described the blocks as 'virtually row houses stacked one on top of another'. Lifts provided access to covered 'sidewalks in the sky' on the north side; these were ten feet wide and open to the elements, being intended to serve as general social spaces, and to give each apartment through natural ventilation.

Worries about who was going to clear away the snow from these north-facing sidewalks may have led to the adoption of the relatively copy-book European scheme built in 1950–60. Ten blocks, of 12-, 13- and 21-storeys, clad in metal curtain-walls, and with internal corridors served by a single bank of lifts, are staggered down the site, and the row houses were omitted.

The ten years from the start of building at Lake Meadows conveniently frame SOM's four canonical buildings of their 'American' period (the dates are those of completion): Lever House, 1952; Manufacturers Hanover Trust, Fifth Avenue Branch, 1954; Connecticut General Life's offices, 1957; and, in 1961, the Chase Manhattan Bank, which closes the decade.[3]

Although difficult, it is just possible, by standing on the corner of the Seagram Building's plaza and looking north-west across Park Avenue, to see Lever House as it appeared in 1952: a small office building[4] whose form and materials disrupted the pattern of tightly built-up masonry of the surrounding blocks. But more important than its power to startle, characteristic of a young architect's first large work (Bunshaft was then in his early forties), the design of Lever House brilliantly gathered together in one building strands of a large number of contradictory European myths and programmatic requirements of Modern Architecture as set out by Johnson and Hitchcock in *The International Style*, and the twin American traditions of the careful re-use of European forms, and the glamour of display: styling.

The building serves as a checklist of those qualities which Hitchcock and Johnson were rash enough to identify in 1932 as qualifying a building for inclusion in the International Style canon: 'a new conception of architecture as volume rather than mass'; 'regularity rather than axial symmetry serves as the chief means of ordering design'; and the proscription of 'arbitrary applied decoration'. The reflecting glass walls clothing the indistinct structure of the tower were a realized part of Modern Architecture's programme from Scheerbart and Taut through Mies and Le Corbusier, but the wrap-round skin with its square corners

—the only places at which the glass is actually transparent—and the blue-green colour of the spandrel which was to persist through the 1950s, were new. Inside, the office spaces are interrupted by an off-centre row of columns, and the flat suspended ceilings house flush light-fittings and air extract grilles.

Shininess had been used at street level both inside and on the outside of Howe and Lescaze's Philadelphia Savings Fund Society building, and the Empire State Building has stainless-steel styling strips set in the stone between the windows and running from top to bottom, but the radical Americanness of the Lever mullions, transoms and facias was enthusiastically recognized by *Architectural Record* in 1952:

> 'There are other buildings in the US which have the same sleek metal and glass excitement . . . the walls of 10,000 diners along the continent's highways. The short-order cooks discovered stainless steel before the architects did. The building seems to say "I am completely expressive of this industrial age: here are columns, office spaces, circulation systems, all visible and obvious." '

Lever, along with the public-spiritedness shown in not building into the whole permitted zoning envelope, reintroduced the idea of the plaza, given away for public use, but here this can now be seen to make no more sense on Park Avenue than Union Carbide's timid set-back further down the same street. As a general pattern for urban form, the directional office slab on a pad of service functions has had disastrous world-wide imitators, and has only been repeated in SOM's own work in the San Francisco Alcoa building (1968), and, in an industrial setting, in the Heinz research laboratories and offices on the banks of the Allegheny River at Pittsburgh (1959).

In the early 1950s, after the completion of Lever House, SOM carried out two buildings which continue the tradition established during the war—that of workmanlike non-architecture: the Heinz vinegar plant, Pittsburgh, Pa (1952), and the Gunners Mates School, Great Lakes, Illinois (1954). Both are exercises in the elegant, flush and, from the outside, opaque skin. The first houses vinegar vats behind the blue glass and red doors, the second a beautifully organized section: the middle third of the plan of a box 240 feet square and 50 feet high is taken up with four floors of classrooms served on either side by galleries which look over voids for crane-runs for the training display and operation of, then, guns, now missiles. These buildings are the beginning of a series of research laboratories, industrial and transport buildings, hospitals, running through SOM's work and complementary to their urban commercial palaces. The banal geometry and simple circulation patterns, and the luxurious detailing of the marble, aluminium and terrazzo finishes, really work when used in transport buildings like the entirely subterranean 2-storey Greyhound Terminal, Chicago (1954), from which the buses are tunnelled directly onto the Dan Ryan Expressway, and O'Hare Airport Terminal, Chicago.

Manufacturers Hanover Trust's branch bank (1953–4) on Fifth Avenue, New York, uses dislocation of the street block as its means of advertising itself (and the sad backs of its neighbours). It appears as a transparent centrally organized pavilion with an envelope that would slip easily into any European city street, but it is really a skin taken round the street block's corner, with servicing accommodation pushed to the back and sides. Pepsi-Cola later played the same game on Park Avenue. All the architectural effort is directed towards exhibiting the magic of the public use of the pavement level and mezzanine banking halls. Here the glass is transparent, internal and external reflections being deliberately controlled and cut down by the all-over suspended illuminated ceilings of fluted plastic which shine through the New York gloom, and through which the columns of a structure—here even more unimportant than at Lever—casually pass. The whole building is carried by its curtains, shiny escalators, finishes, and Harry Bertoia's flashy mural, and the vestigial old-style architecture resides in a skin composed of what now look like large aluminium shop-fitting sections with exposed screwed bead-fixings.

SOM's rural Mustang[5] was launched in 1957: that year's model was called the Connecticut General Life Insurance Company's headquarters at Bloomfield outside Hartford—three differentiated buildings neoplastically arranged in 280 acres of landscaping. Eero Saarinen had earlier canonized the idea of the pastoral corporation headquarters at General Motors ('Where today meets tomorrow'), completed in 1955. After the usual, for SOM, comprehensive study of the company's needs, and the making of a full-size (72 × 60 feet) mock-up, they produced in one of the three buildings their basic country palazzo, a model which is still being restyled after twelve years.[6] The main palace has three storeys and a basement, four Noguchi-decorated courts alternating with slim cores of services; the building beautifully organizes the office hierarchy with its general offices on the outside separated by the cores from the smaller cells, which look onto the courts. Similar office organization research for Ford's headquarters at Dearborn, Michigan, built at the same time, produced a quite conventional form, but insurance executives were found to require a 6 ft office module, compared with Ford's 4 ft 8 in. A suspended ceiling was not used: instead the space is used in depth, divided up into bays by vertical, acoustically absorbent, perforated-metal screens, each bay housing a bare fluorescent tube. The verticals provide cut-off from glare, and their intersections form fixing points for the posts of the movable partitions. The styling of the buildings' skins closely follows the subdivisions of Pietro Belluschi's Equitable Savings and Loan Building, Portland, Oregon, finished in 1948.

With this banal beaux-arts *parti*, SOM had re-invented a building form which could be used in practically any non-urban situation, any climate, and for any function. Given these advantages, and the magic appeal of the buildings for American-admiring businessmen, it may seem surprising that they have produced few world-wide copies, until it is realized that the form, in its necessary rural setting, requires a mainly car-owning work force: that it remains essentially American.

'The water-locked snout of land [the Wall Street area] now boasts the biggest commercial office building constructed anywhere in more than a quarter of a century.'[7]

With a staggering expenditure of 96 million dollars, the completion in 1962 of the 60-storey headquarters of the Chase Manhattan Bank in downtown New York marks the climax and close of what has here been

14

called SOM's American period; the building in which the cultural aspirations of Lever House are confidentially achieved. As in Lever, dislocation is the starting point, here not just of a street or a block, but of the entire built form of the 'water-locked snout', and the remembered image of the Staten Island Ferry view. It is a directional slab 90 feet thick in an irregular street pattern; ribbed with external columns, shiny, repetitive, and flat topped, taller than the stone-covered, articulated and pointy towers in which it is set. (SOM have subsequently dislocated their own dislocation by building a flush brown tower—the Marine Grace Insurance building—immediately next door to the west.)

The 2½-acre plaza, formed by throwing together two blocks and keeping the service platform on which the tower stands low, works for the pedestrian where Lever's does not: providing real space, hawthorn trees, a Noguchi-decorated hole, and a clear view of the sky and its reflection in the building, in the otherwise medieval surroundings. But the apotheosis of SOM's style is found *inside* the building in three of the areas for which the firm's interior design division were responsible, and through which 'a dozen young ladies trained to give tours in ten languages' guide the tourist visitor. A tour of the underground banking hall and concourse in the platform, the individually tailored vice-presidential offices of the 17th floor and the executive suites on the 60th, disturbs the non-American now as violently as in Imperial Rome the newly finished Baths of Caracalla would have disturbed a visiting colonial Greek. All these rooms have the specifically Roman sense of an all-out bid for culture, however eclectic. *Interiors*, in its review, conveys the breathlessness of that bid and its achievement so well that its description acts as a metaphor for the whole building:

'Unlike most interiors by SOM which seem to have dropped into the 20th century disattached from the past, the Chase offices evince a sense of history. There are antiques in these interiors, there are ancient sculptures and ceramics, an early American ship's figurehead, ornate old picture frames. And many of the modern furniture designs, some by SOM, . . . are of a form and spirit that suggest a continuity with past cultures. . . [They] are treated as *more* than a continuity of the architecture. They possess a rich interest and even splendor in themselves. [The] lavish abundance of wall materials include silks, teak, German oak, French walnut, plastics, plaster, paint, a variety of marbles and woods and lacquers for desks and cabinets, a veritable parade of textured fabrics and leather colors.'

The description finishes by listing some of the treasures in the half-million dollar collection of paintings and sculptures, included in which are all Bunshaft's favourites: Calder, Miró, Bertoia.

An architect-engineer, Myron Goldsmith, called to the San Francisco office in 1958 by William B. Dunlap, is responsible for the spectacular further development of the non-architectural side of the SOM practice in the 1960s.[8] Goldsmith, brought up in Chicago, had enrolled at Illinois Institute of Technology (IIT) in the late 1930s and graduated in architecture in 1939, but with training sufficient to qualify also as an engineer. During the war he worked in the U.S. Navy's Bureau of Yards and Docks as engineer, but afterwards for Mies van der Rohe until 1953, this time broken by nine months spent travelling in Europe. Mies' office produced during this period Promontory Apartments, 860 Lake Shore Drive, buildings at the IIT campus, and entered the Mannheim Theatre competition. From 1953 Goldsmith spent two years at the University of Rome, on a Fulbright Fellowship, with Pier Luigi Nervi, and during this time worked with James Ferris on three projects; one, with Bruno Zevi, was a competition entry for the Garibaldi bridge in Rome, which shows the development of a flaring, tapering structure in both the road and its articulated supports. As part of his Master's thesis for IIT, Goldsmith had studied 'the tall building', producing designs for an 86-storey prestressed concrete tower with a giant order of profiled columns placed outside the envelope, and a scheme for external diagonal wind-bracing.

The hangars for servicing and washing United Air Lines' DC8 fleet at San Francisco airport were the largest engineering job which SOM had up till then been asked to design, and, in 1958 SOM's office there asked Goldsmith to join them as head of the structural department. The plan of the hangar closely resembles that of the Gunners' Mates School, but here the profiled concrete-framed core, omitted in places to accommodate the noses of the planes, is used as a root from which to cantilever the steel structure of the roof. The drive-in plane-wash hangar is a beautiful exercise in skinned-down welded-steel portal frame-construction and the 43 ft high notch in the gable ends, allowing the tail-plane of a DC8 to pass through, is a poignant reminder of the rate of aircraft obsolescence. Because of a shortage of large-scale work after completion of the hangars, Goldsmith soon moved in 1959 to the Chicago office.

'Window and pier fenestration—a new trend?' asked a headline in *Architectural Record* in 1955. There is a danger in histories of architecture written at such short range of looking for causalities which may later turn out to be spurious, or to have been deliberately engineered by the protagonists. However, in the last years of the Eisenhower administration, the middle and end of the 1950s, before Chase Manhattan's foundations were being laid, it became obvious that a major lurch had taken place in the direction of American architecture: that the apparent consensus—exemplified in Bunshaft's belief in buildings as rectangular, repetitive, smooth and shiny, their functions housed in an easy unarticulated way, helped by banal geometry—was being deliberately overturned.

Five American buildings from this period contain the seeds of what was to follow in the next ten years, and can be taken now as exemplars of the upheaval. From the older generation, Eero Saarinen (b. 1910) turned from the styling of General Motors to the specific, closed forms of the Kresge Auditorium and the Chapel at Massachusetts Institute of Technology, Cambridge, Mass. (1955). Mies van der Rohe and Philip Johnson's Seagram building was finished in 1958. In Massachusetts Paul Rudolph (b. 1919) designed Wellesley College's neo-neo-Gothic Cultural Center in 1955 (completed in 1959). And SOM in the same year completed the John Hancock Mutual Life Insurance Company building at San Francisco, and two years later the First City National Bank, Houston, Texas.[9]

After the Crown Zellerbach headquarters, completed in 1959, SOM's San Francisco office's second large West coast commission, the John Hancock building, has the distinction of being the first and, until now, only one of the firm's buildings which cannot be classified under Hitchcock and Johnson's criteria as belonging to the International Style. The American development of the architecture of the Heroic Period, started in earnest by SOM with Lever House, has come to an end. The Hancock building is a squat, 120-ft square bilaterally symmetrical tower, a solid with holes in walls apparently made of huge granite lumps articulated from each other like rusticated stones. Its *parti* is Sullivan revival: a base, middle and cornice; but each element, concrete, granite and concrete, seems to have been designed separately from the other, and the result is like a game of architectural 'Consequences'. An attempt is made to *demonstrate* the acceptance of load from the walls above onto the segmentally arched collecting beam by the concrete *pilotis*, in a way quite different from that in which columns either simply emerge at the base from behind the skins of the earlier buildings, or are of no formal consequence in the planning.

The First City National Bank, Houston, Texas (1961), launched a stylistically identifiable series of buildings for the 1960s: office towers, each getting progressively larger on plan, and with an increasing economy in structure and service cores. In this complex of buildings (tower, single-storey banking hall on one block, and parking building on an adjacent one) the skin of the offices (grey glass set in aluminium) is set back behind the bones of the external columns and edge-beams of the steel frame which is itself faced in white Vermont marble. The setting-back of the skin has, in southerly Texas, the technical justification of reducing both the load on air-conditioning equipment, caused by the sun's heat, and glare from inside, and of helping window cleaning—problems which do not, however, seem to have been insuperable in their earlier glass-covered buildings. These can also be seen as the first symptom of SOM's increasing reliance during the 1960s on the structural scheme of a building to produce, later to *become*, its form. In the transitional group, both the previous 'American' style of the single-storey banking hall with its structure inside, and the new structuralism of the office tower are uneasily thrown together on the same block.

The history of SOM's designs from the completion of First City National Bank to those of the present is generally one of an increasing obsession with structure, and increasingly more rigid Beaux Arts plans. A law of diminishing returns seems to have been operating, requiring each successive building to exhibit and demonstrate more forcefully the anthropomorphic qualities of structure, for example at John Hancock in the profiling of the *pilotis* to show how the forces might be transferred from above to the ground. (United Air Lines' offices, Myron Goldsmith's first engineered building at the Chicago office, is in spite of later necessary modifications a major, cool exception.) The Hartford Fire Insurance Company's office, Chicago, nine by seven bays, but otherwise following the pattern of the First City National Bank, develops little shear-resisting splays at the ends of beams where these meet the columns.

These, in retrospect, tentative structural profilings seem to have been the cue for a flurry of buildings which showed not only tapers and profiling of the exposed structural frame, but a determination to leave on the finished building evidence of the way in which the structural pieces had been assembled. The Banque Lambert headquarters, Brussels (1958–64), SOM's first large European commission,[10] and carried out by the New York office, represents the flowering of this style, and the one in which SOM's own confidence in their American style seems to have been shaken. The tapered precast concrete crosses of the frame are joined and isolated from each other by shiny stainless-steel plates and bosses. In trying to provide usable public space by setting back the building from the pavement all round the block, and by making it slightly too tall for its immediate neighbours to achieve European-style 'infill' successfully, every one of Eero Saarinen's later urbanistic failures (in European terms, in Grosvenor Square at the U.S. Embassy, London) are strangely anticipated.

In the last half of the 1960s—during which the firm has built such disparate works as the cool Boots Pure Drug offices at Nottingham, England, the vulgar San Francisco Alcoa headquarters and various travertine-covered towers in Chicago, continuing both their all-metal and masonry styles—it becomes increasingly difficult to regard the work of SOM's various offices at New York, San Francisco, Chicago and Portland as having a homogeneity other than that provided by the umbrella of the name. The continued articulation of structural form has been the characteristic of all work since the Banque Lambert, and occasionally this beautifully meshes with the function, as in the covered and open arenas of the Oakland-Alameda County Coliseum, California, finished in 1967. More often, though, it has led to the structural megalomania of the Cor-ten steel John Hancock tower in Chicago, and the Alcoa headquarters where the diagonal bracing has taken over the elevations (this is explained in the San Francisco building as combining the advantages of a stiff truss to reduce sway, and a flexible moment-resisting frame to absorb earthquake forces). The first-floor collecting beam of the earlier John Hancock building has reappeared in giant form, together with references to the splayed base of the Monadnock building (Burnham and Root, 1893), and in the Brunswick Corporation's building in Chicago (1965) where it requires columns nine feet square at pavement level to support it.

The model of the project for the Chicago campus of the University of Illinois, to serve 20,000 students, shows buildings organized by function rather than faculty, in an unresolved combination of axial and neoplastic arrangements, their styling similar to that of the Hartford Fire Insurance offices. The finished works, however, in a misguided attempt to produce variety, seem to have absorbed all the decorative and structuralist clichés of post-war European building (board-marked rough concrete in Chicago is as anomalous as a Fiat 500).

SOM, especially in their work of the 1950s, have demonstrated that in America it has been quite possible to make architecture without most of those components conventionally considered necessary in Europe. In doing so they transcended earlier criteria for what makes modern buildings: the definition of architecture then expands to include these tenuous buildings. More importantly, they had shown, before the watershed of Hancock in San Francisco, that the symbolic functions of a building could be carried by its graphics, finishes or artworks—its decorations—

and that Architecture may not necessarily be, and probably is not, one of the chief media of American culture.

The New York Museum of Modern Art's catalogue of its exhibition of SOM's work there in 1950 stated that the firm 'produces imaginative, serviceable and sophisticated architecture deserving of special attention . . . animated by the discipline of modern methods'. Henry Russell Hitchcock[11] thought in 1961 that these methods would become increasingly accepted throughout the Western world, but this cannot now generally be held true. (The only other comparably large architectural organization, the Architect's Department of the Greater London Council—formerly London County Council, has since withered away as the result of decentralizing legislation.)

SOM's work is now most successful and convincing in two areas: in their modest servicing and transport buildings; and in embodying and reflecting the values of the large American hierarchical institutions of commerce and defence which their own organization has grown up to emulate. But, as it is precisely these institutions which are at present under siege in the United States, no predictions should here be made for the next decade.

1 The Seagram Building, 375 Park Avenue, New York (1958)

2 The site population consisted of 3,500 families, of whom 1,400 could be rehoused at the new lower density, but of the existing occupants it was estimated that only 10–15% would be able to afford the rents for the new apartments. Another 25% would be eligible for public housing. This was the first large housing group intended primarily for Negroes to be sponsored by an insurance company.

3 The Union Carbide building in Park Avenue, finished before Chase Manhattan in 1960, is not included in this group, as although the immaculate interior fitting-out marks a climax in SOM's use of all-over modular illuminated ceilings and movable partition systems, and the façades are not covered in stones, the overall plan and envelope and the tidy square-bay structures seem Seagram-influenced, and belong to the next decade.

4 Small in size—21 storeys plus plant, and small on plan—53 × 180 feet; no desk is more than 25 feet from a window. The vast matrix of desks which faced Jack Lemmon in the film 'The Apartment' was to come only later, at the end of the 1950s.

5 In Britain, the Ford Capri perhaps is an equivalent, with its choice of engine size and optional 'clip-on customizing packs'.

6 Later models: 1958, Reynolds Metal, Richmond, Va (with added sun-control); 1961, Upjohn Pharmaceuticals, Kalamazoo, Mich. (steel and space-frame roof); 1962, Cadet Housing and Library, U.S. Air Force Academy, Colorado Springs (on a platform); 1963, United Air Lines, Des Plaines, Ill. (square, prestressed concrete), and Emhart Manufacturing, Bloomfield, Conn. (profiled concrete and *pilotis*); 1966, Heinz offices, Uxbridge, Middlesex, England (profiled concrete); 1968, Boots offices, Beeston, Nottingham, England (steel).

7 Guidebook, '1 Chase Manhattan Plaza'.

8 Goldsmith might also be thought responsible for SOM's developing structural-ism discussed below, but for the facts that the New York office's Banque Lambert, Brussels, had been designed before his arrival, and that the idea for the Hartford Insurance building's façade had been invented by Bruce Graham in the Chicago office for an unbuilt project for a hotel on the Loop for Herbert Greenwald (Mies' great client). It seems possible, however, that the general interest in structure as form generator may be the result of the first generations of students trained under Mies and Hilberseimer at IIT beginning to make themselves felt in working offices. The buildings which SOM themselves are now carrying out at IIT show just how good (extensions to Minerals and Metallurgy building) and how bad (Library and Administration building) followers of Mies can be.

9 In association with Wilson, Morris, Crain and Anderson

10 In Germany the firm had built the U.S. Consulate, Dusseldorf, and housing for the U.S. State Department, Bremen, in 1954–5.

11 Introduction to Ernst Danz, *Architecture of SOM 1950–62* (London, 1963)

The Plates

Bruce Graham

John Hancock Center, Chicago, Ill.
(1968)

**1-6, Lever House,
Park Avenue, New York
(1951-52)**

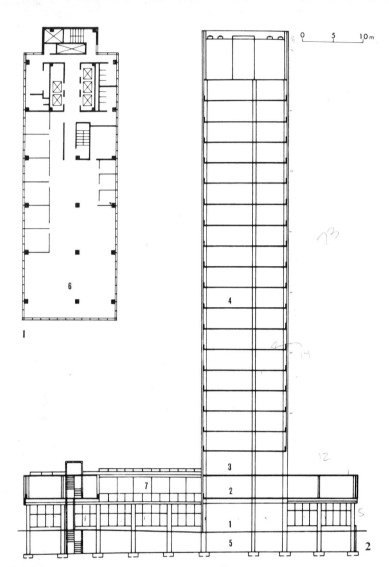

1, 2 Plan (left) of typical office
floor, and section: 1, entrance hall;
2, assembly room; 3, dining room;
4, office floor; 5, basement; 6,
offices; 7, open court

3 Court and dining room terrace

4 General view across Park
Avenue

5 Foot of tower from across court

6 Detail of the tower curtain-wall

3

**7-11, Manufacturers Hanover Trust Company,
Fifth Avenue, New York (1953-54)**

Gordon Bunshaft

7 Part of the main elevation to
Fifth Avenue

8, 9 Plans of the public banking
halls (left, mezzanine; right,
ground floor): 1, entrance; 2,
banking hall; 3, safe; 4, escalators;
5, tellers' counter; 6, banking hall;
7, screen; 8, lift lobby

10 View across Fifth Avenue

11 Tellers' counter, and screen by
Harry Bertoia

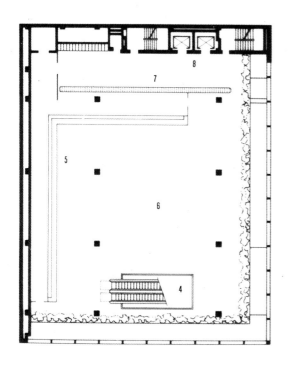

8

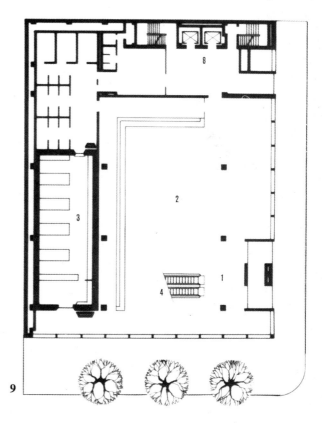

9

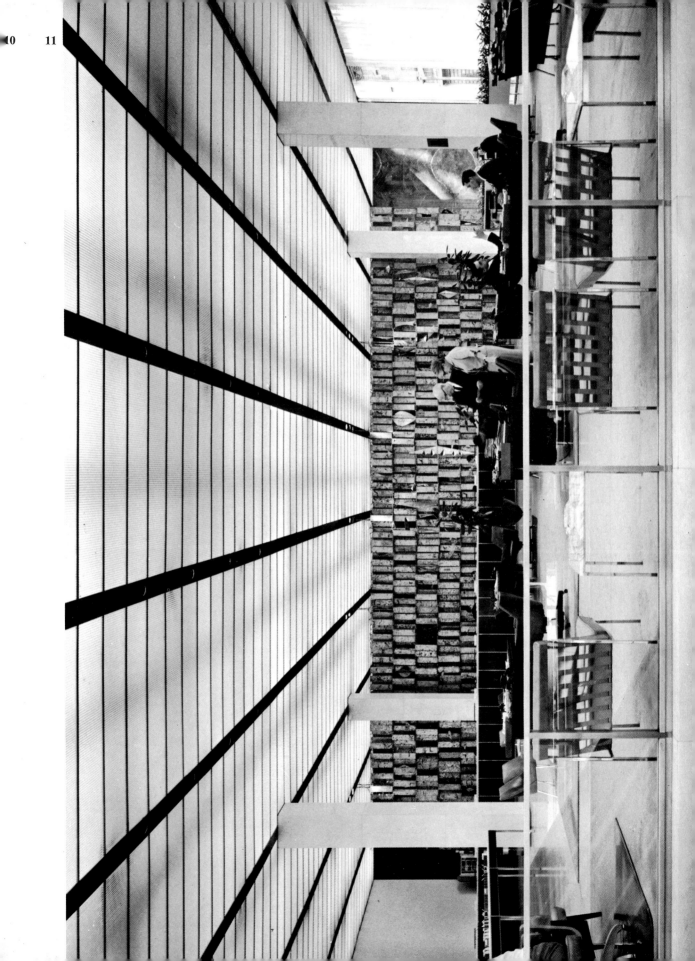

12-14, Inland Steel Company headquarters building, West Monroe St, Chicago, Ill. (1956-58)

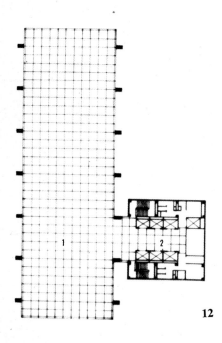

12

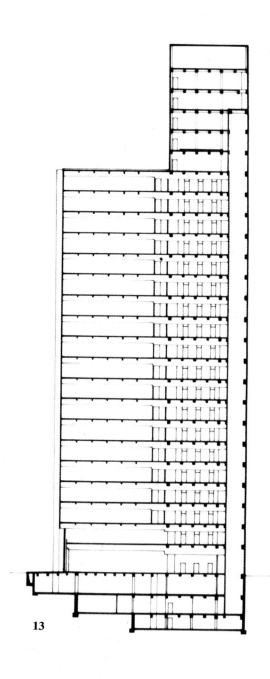

13

12, 13 Plan and short section:
1, general office space; 2, lift lobby

14 General view

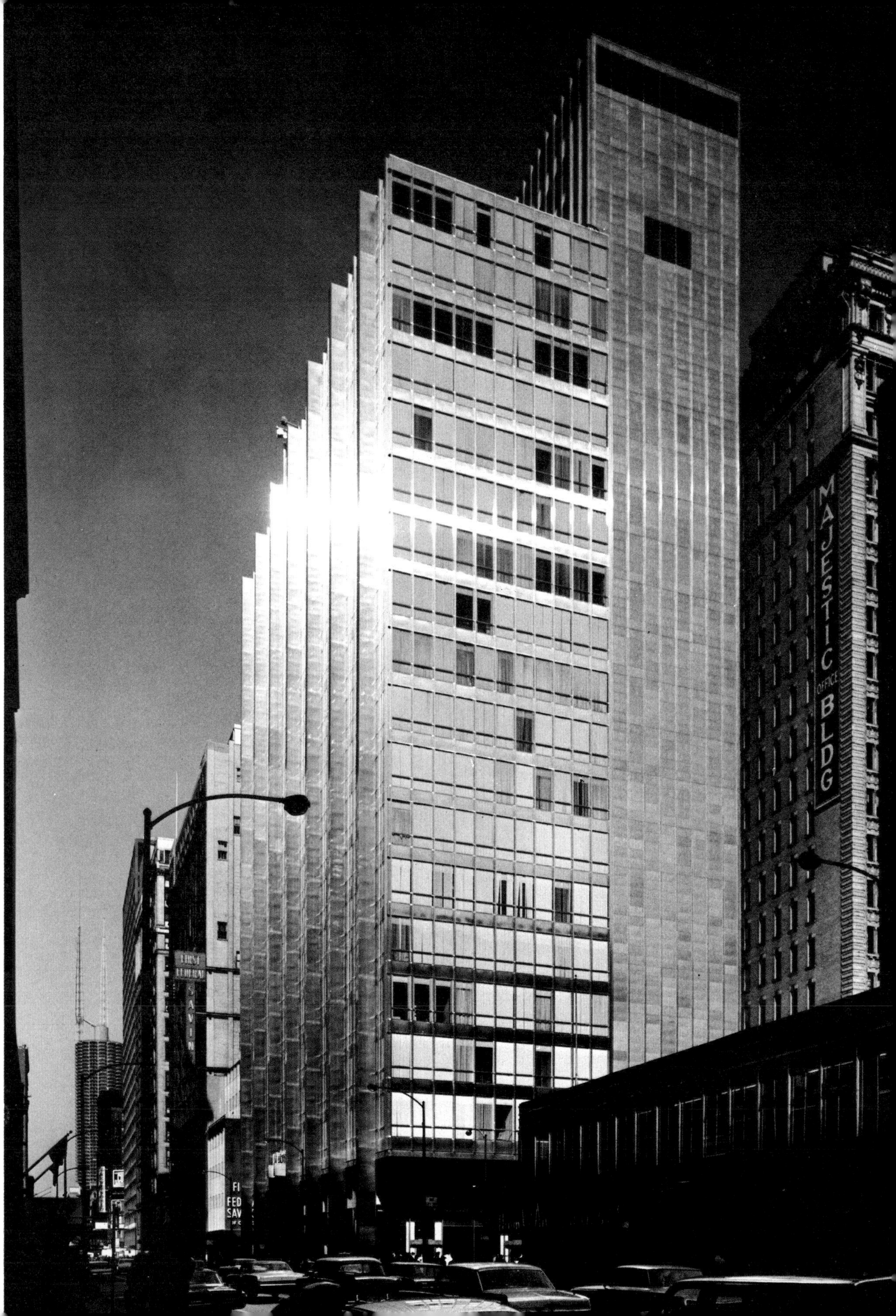
MAJESTIC OFFICE BLDG

**15-17, Pepsi-Cola Company offices
Park Avenue, New York (1958-59)**

Gordon Bumshaft

15, 16 Plans of the Pepsi-Cola building (left, typical office floor; right, ground floor): 1, entrance hall and exhibition space; 2, plant room; 3, general office space; 4, lavatories

17 General view from Park Avenue

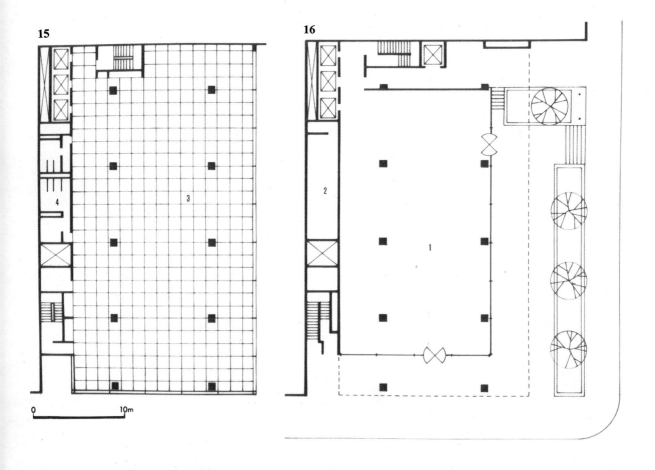

15

16

0   10m

17

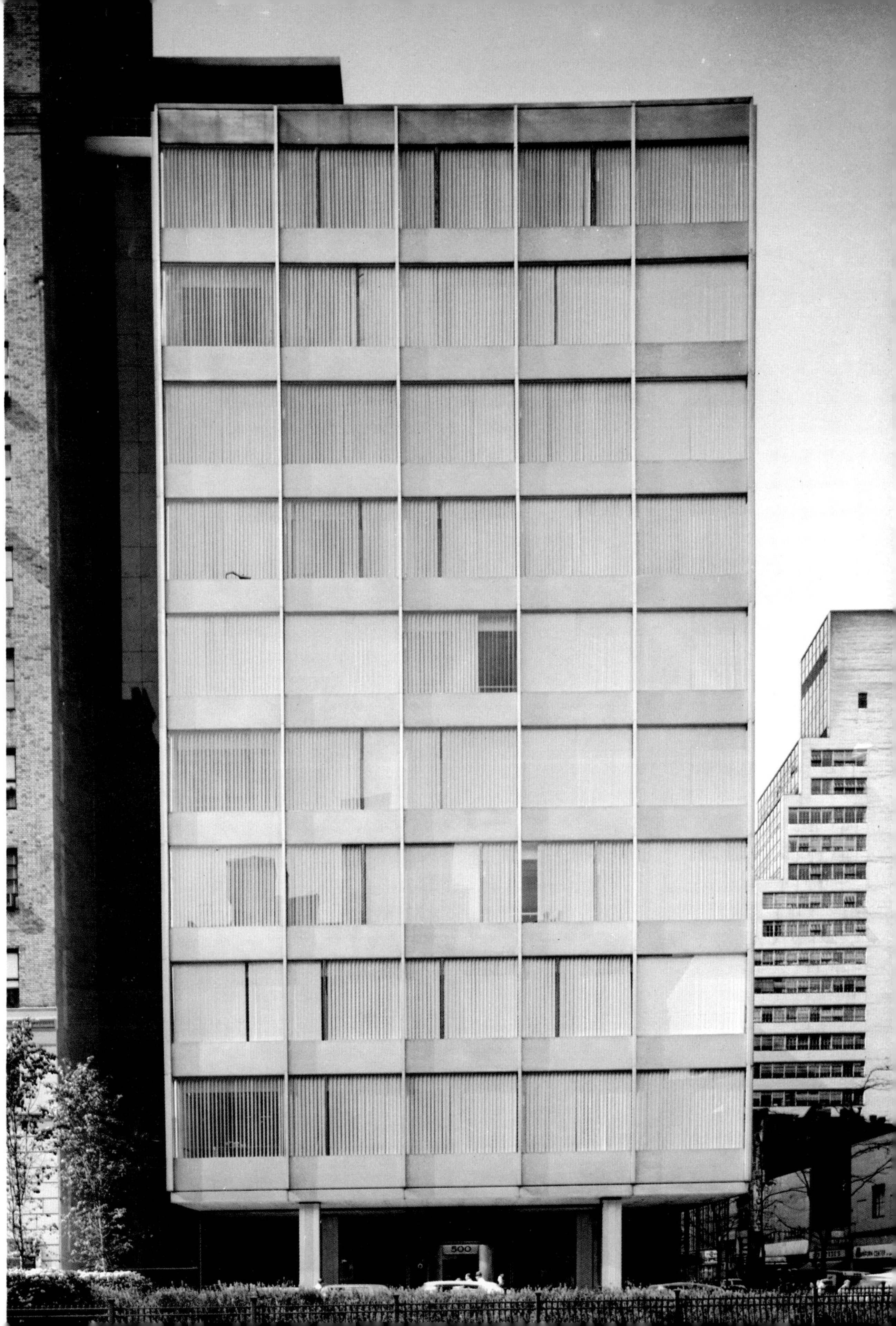

**18-25, U.S. Air Force Academy,
Colorado Springs, Col. (1956-62)**

Walter Netsch

18 General site plan, showing:
1, administration building; 2, social
centre; 3, chapel; 4, cadet living
quarters; 5, library, classrooms and
laboratories; 6, dining hall; 7,
court

19 General view of the Academy

18

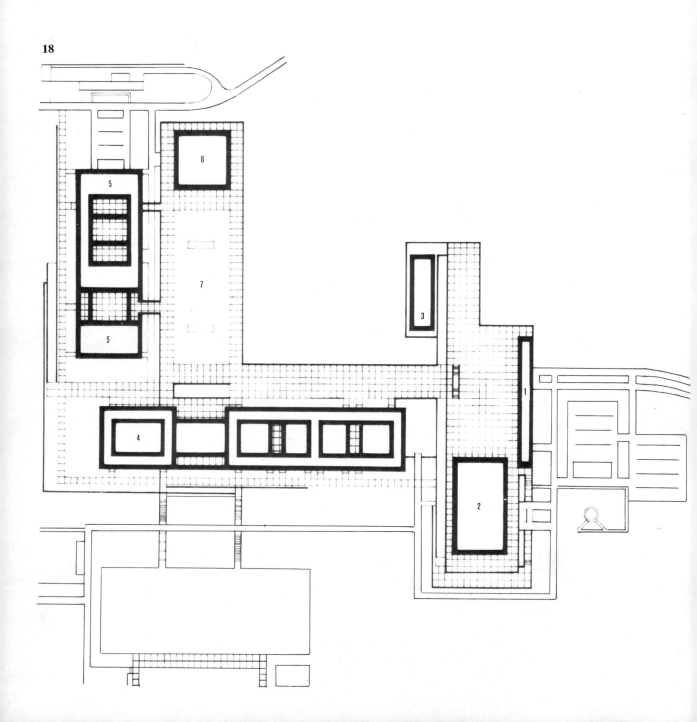

20 Chapel from the lower court

21 Cadet living quarters

22 Short section through chapel: 1, Type A tetrahedron; 2, Type B tetrahedron; 3, Type C tetrahedron; 4, concrete pier; 5, Protestant chapel; 6, Roman Catholic chapel; 7, ramp; 8, basement

23, 24 Plans of chapel (above, ground floor; below, upper floor): 1, entrance; 2, Roman Catholic chapel; 3, Synagogue; 4, Protestant chapel; 5, altar

25 Interior of upper floor of chapel

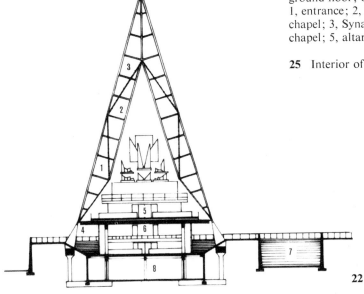

22

23, 24

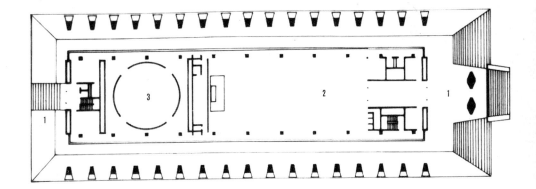

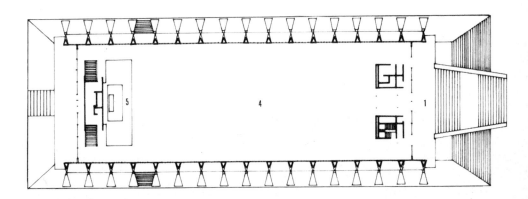

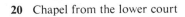

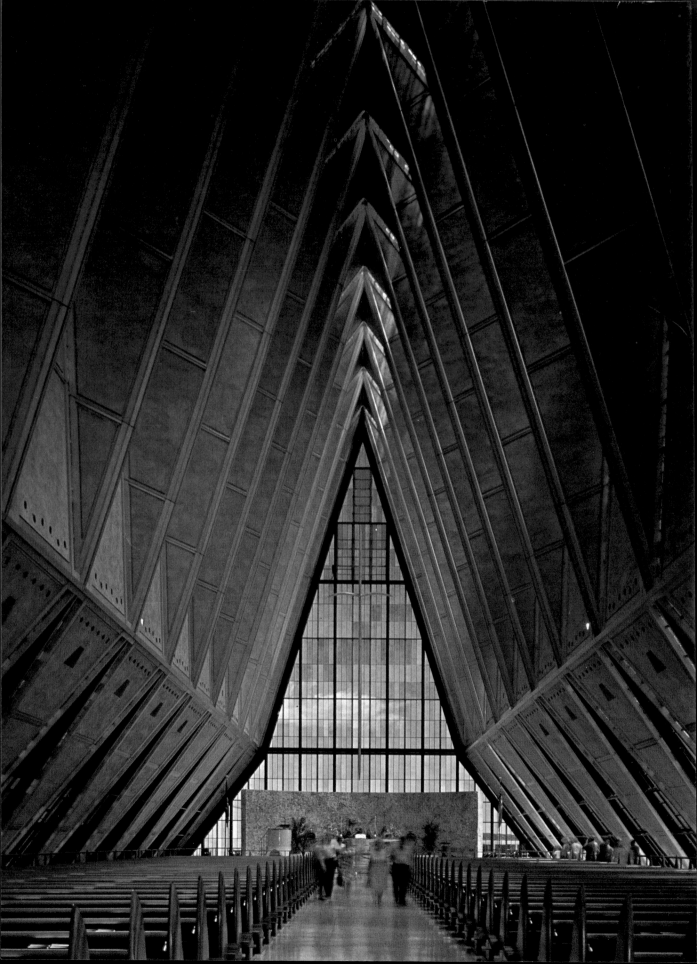

**26, 27, Gunners' Mates School,
Great Lakes, Ill. (1952-54)**

26 Section, showing: 1, classrooms;
2, practical demonstration and
training areas; 3, travelling cranes

27 General view, showing main
entrance to central area and (left)
entrance for equipment

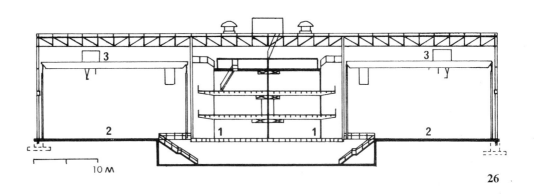

10 M

26

27

28, H. J. Heinz Company, Warehouse and Vinegar Plant, Pittsburgh, Pa (1950-52)

Gordon Bunshaft

28

29, 30, Connecticut General Life Insurance Company, Bloomfield, Conn. (1954-57)

29 Main entrance to the smaller office building, with part of principal building at left

30 Canopied entrance from car park to principal office building seen from an office in the smaller building

31-36, Crown Zellerbach Corporation, headquarters building, San Francisco, Calif. (1957-59)

31 Site plan, showing: 1, entrance hall platform; 2, service tower; 3, branch bank; 4, fountain; 5, car ramp to garage

32 General view of service stack and office tower

33 Entrance hall seen from fountain

34 Entrance hall

35 Plaza and the circular Wells Fargo branch bank

36 *Pilotis* of entrance, and bank

31

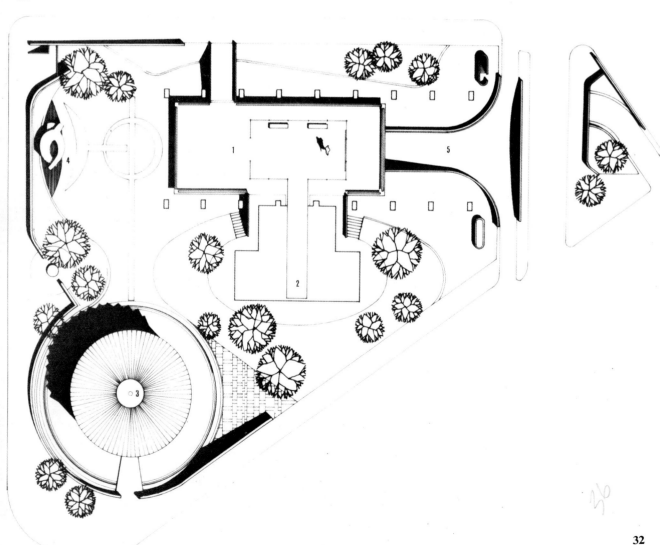

**37-39, Union Carbide
Corporation administrative
offices, Park Avenue,
New York (1957-60)**

38

37 Detail of elevation to Park
Avenue

38 General view of office tower
from street (partly obscured by
neighbouring office building)

39 Plan of ground floor: 1, reception areas on either side of central
service core

0   30m

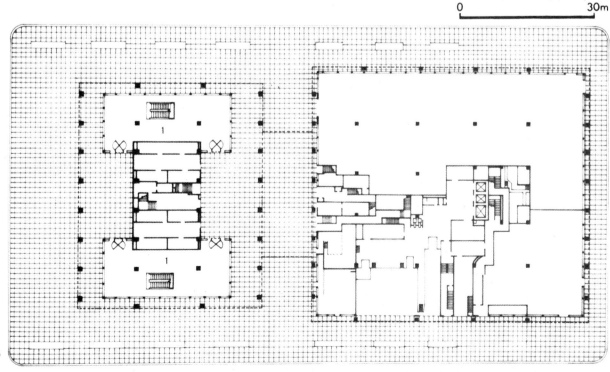

37   39

**40, 41, Harris Trust and Savings Bank offices,
Chicago, Ill. (1957-60)**

40 Ground-floor plan: A,
new office tower; B, existing bank;
C, redesigned office space. Key: 1,
entrance; 2, tellers' counter; 3, loan
department; 4, credit department;
5, office; 6, escalators

41 Tower (set-back machine room
at eleventh floor)

40

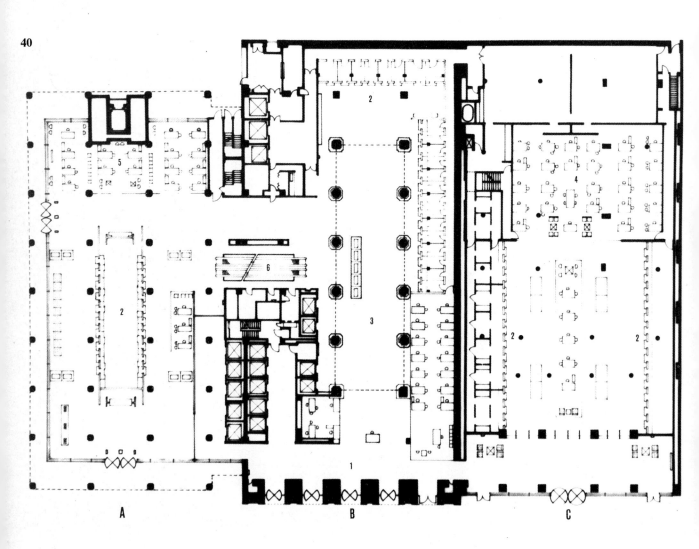

A   B   C

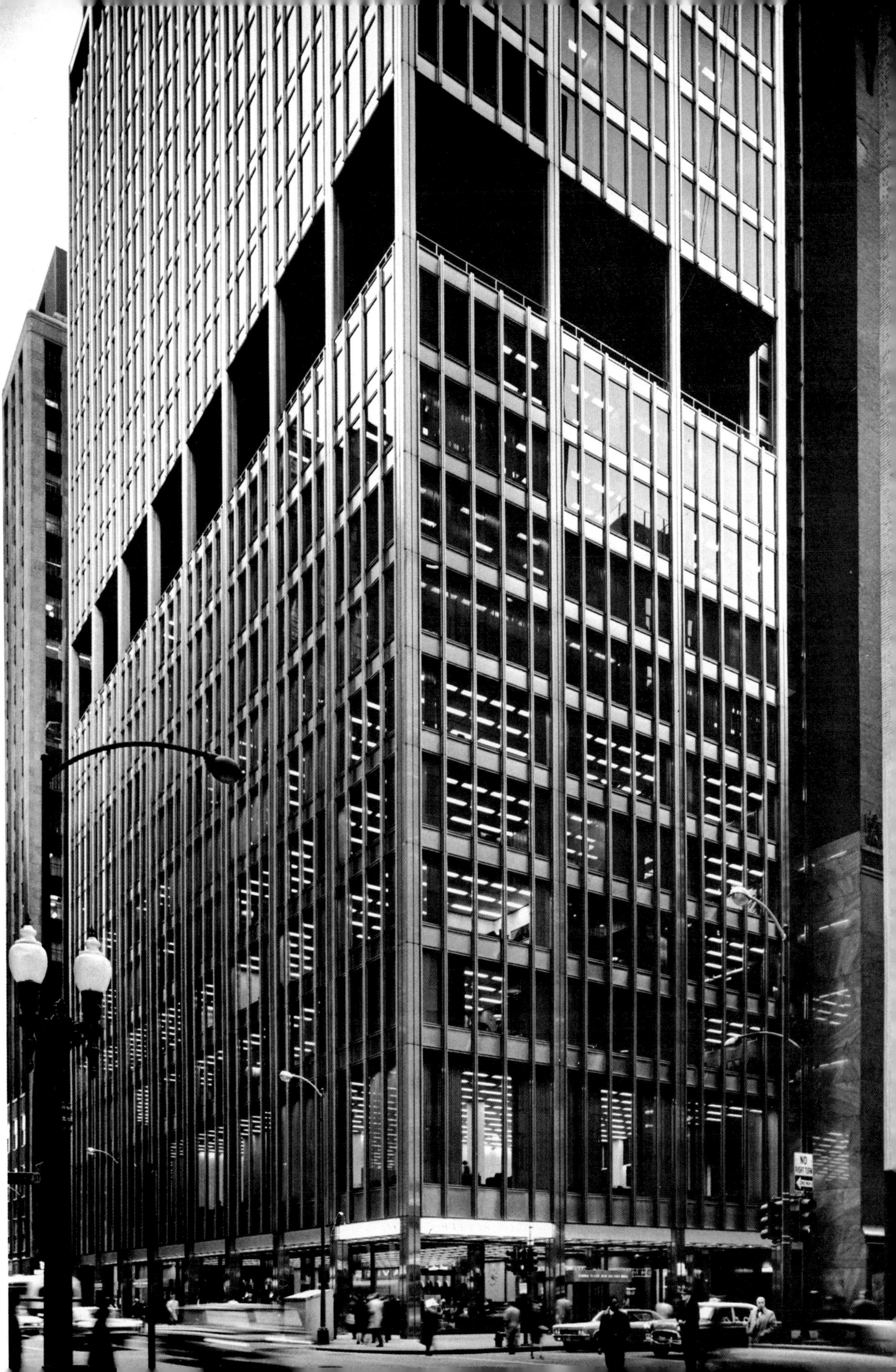

41

42-45, First City National Bank, branch bank and offices, Houston, Texas (1959-61)

42, 43 Plans of (left) typical office floor, and (right) ground floor: 1, banking hall; 2, offices; 3, escalators; 4, tellers' counter; 5, office; 6, drive-in bank; 7, office tower entrance hall; 8, service core; 9, escalators; 10, conference room; 11, office space

44 Façade of the tower, and banking hall (drive-in counters in foreground)

45 Banking hall

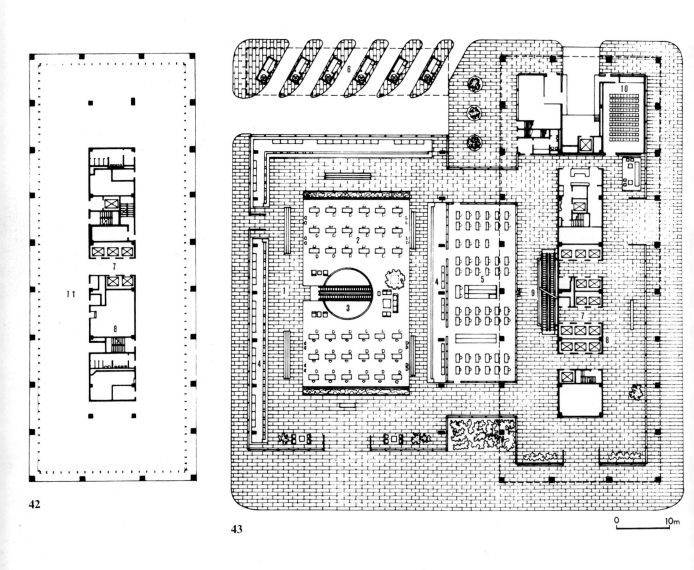

42

43

0   10m

44

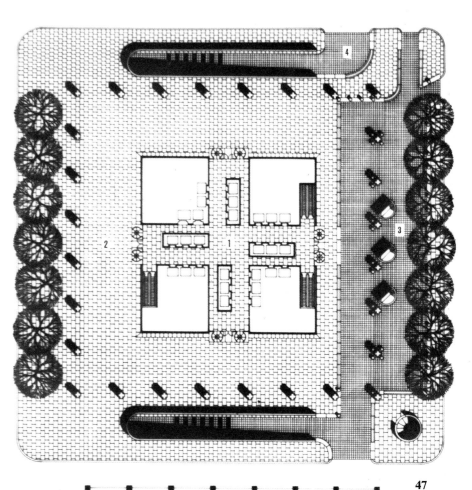

47

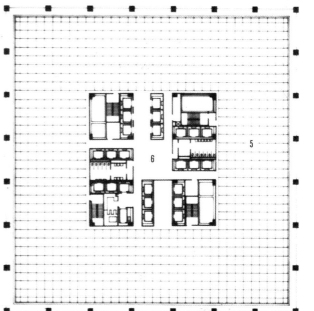

46   General view

47, 48   Plans of (above)
ground floor, and (below) typical
office floor: 1, lift lobby; 2, space
under *pilotis*; 3, plaza; 4, car ramp
to garage; 5, office space; 6, service
core

49   Detail of skin and sun-control
elements

50   View of mezzanine banking
hall under *pilotis*

48

Gordon Bunshaft

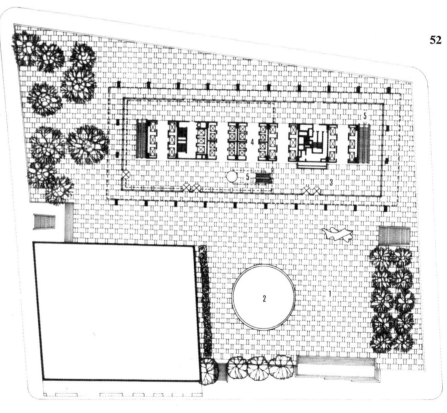

52

51 Wall Street area from the air, Chase Manhattan Bank in centre

52 Site plan, showing: 1, plaza; 2, open court; 3, entrance hall; 4, lift lobbies; 5, escalators

53 Entrance hall under *pilotis* with, below, circular court to banking hall

51

54

56

55

54 Public concourse at pavement level below plaza

55 Executive dining room on 60th floor

56 View from banking hall through court to plaza

**57-64, Upjohn Company
headquarters offices,
Kalamazoo, Mich. (1959-61)**

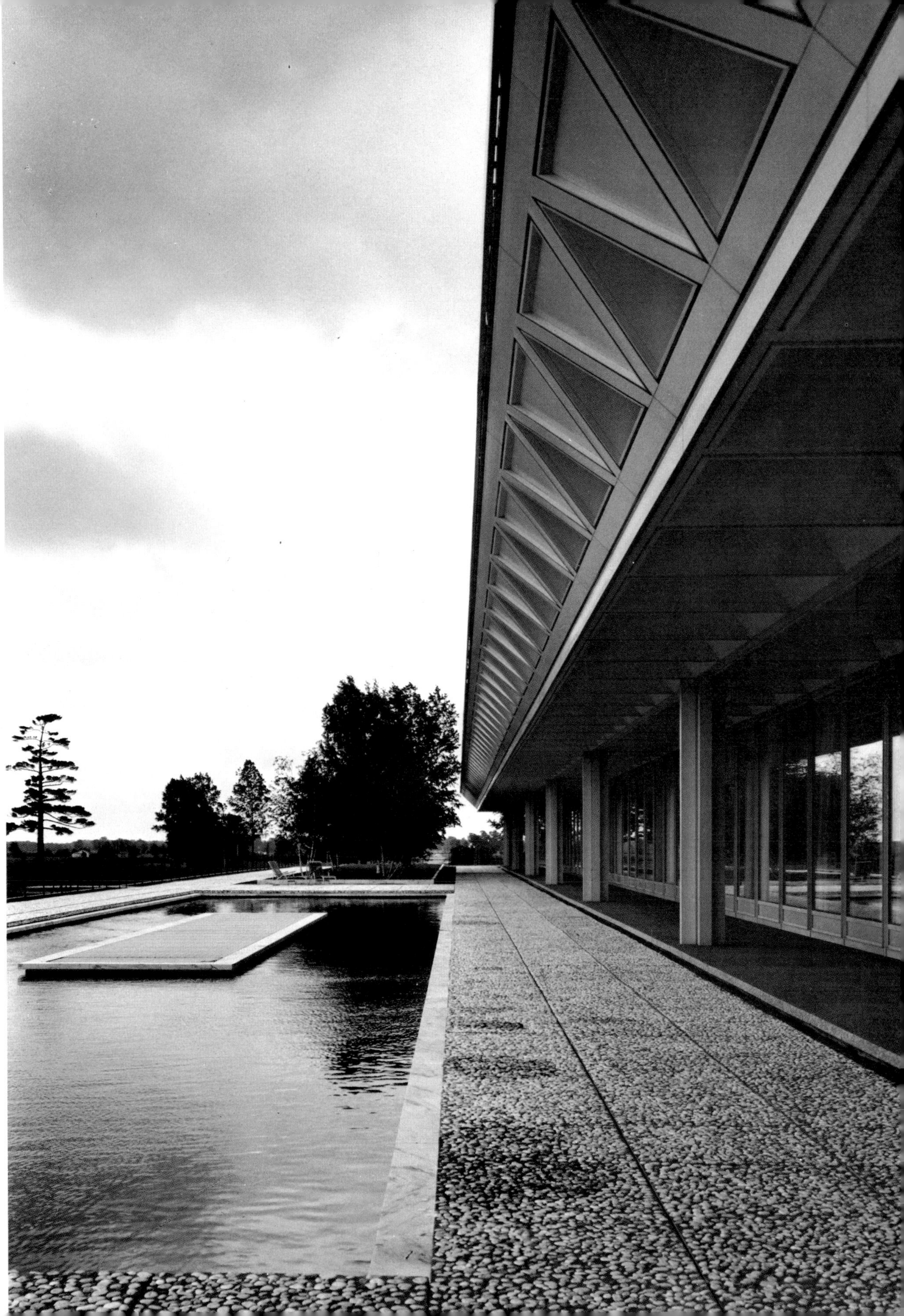

61, 62 Plan, showing: 1, court; 2, escalators; 3, service core; 4, conference room; 5, typical office; 6, lounge. Below, section

63 Dining hall and court

64 Entrance hall

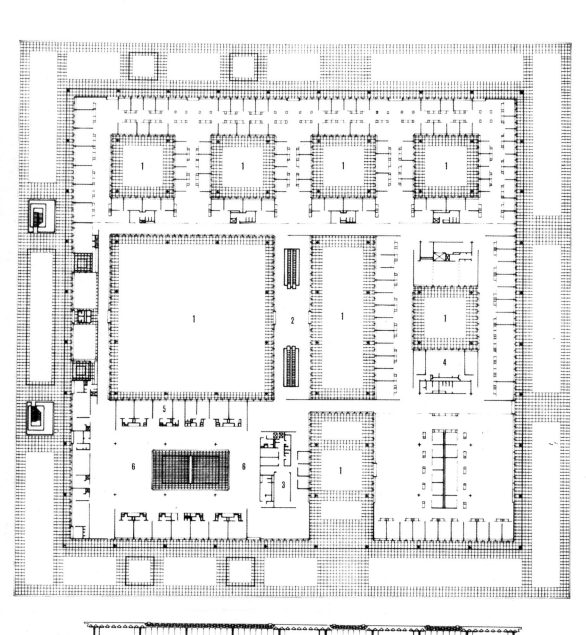

61

62

63 64

65-69, Emhart Manufacturing Company, administration and research building, Bloomfield, Conn. (1963)

65   General view

66   Section

67   Column and cantilevered corner

68   Vehicular entrance court

69   Entrance hall

65

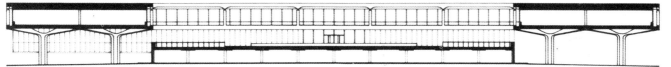

66

70-73, Banque Lambert, Brussels (1964)

70 General view of long elevation

71 Ground-floor plan: 1, entrance; 2, banking hall; 3, lettable offices

72 Raised entrance platform and sculpture by Henry Moore

73 Detail of main elevation showing precast concrete elements

70

71

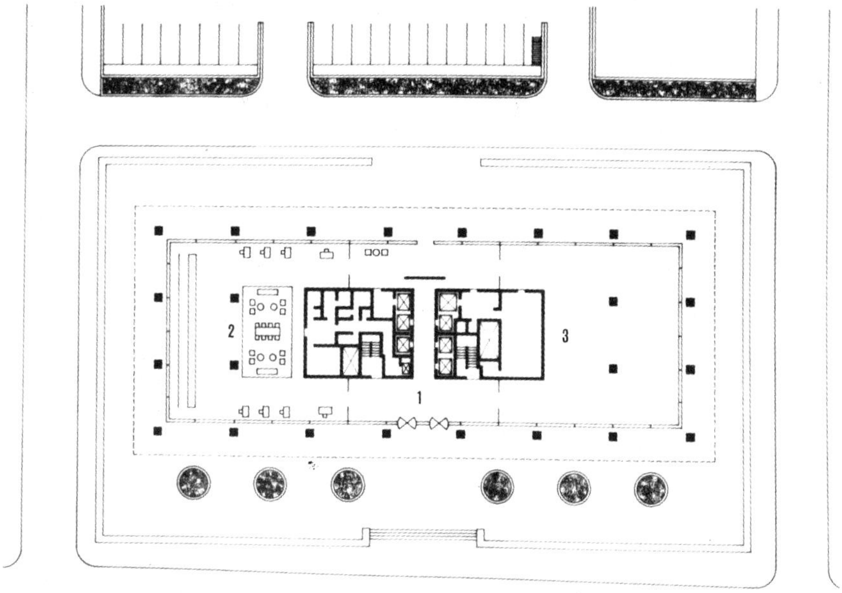

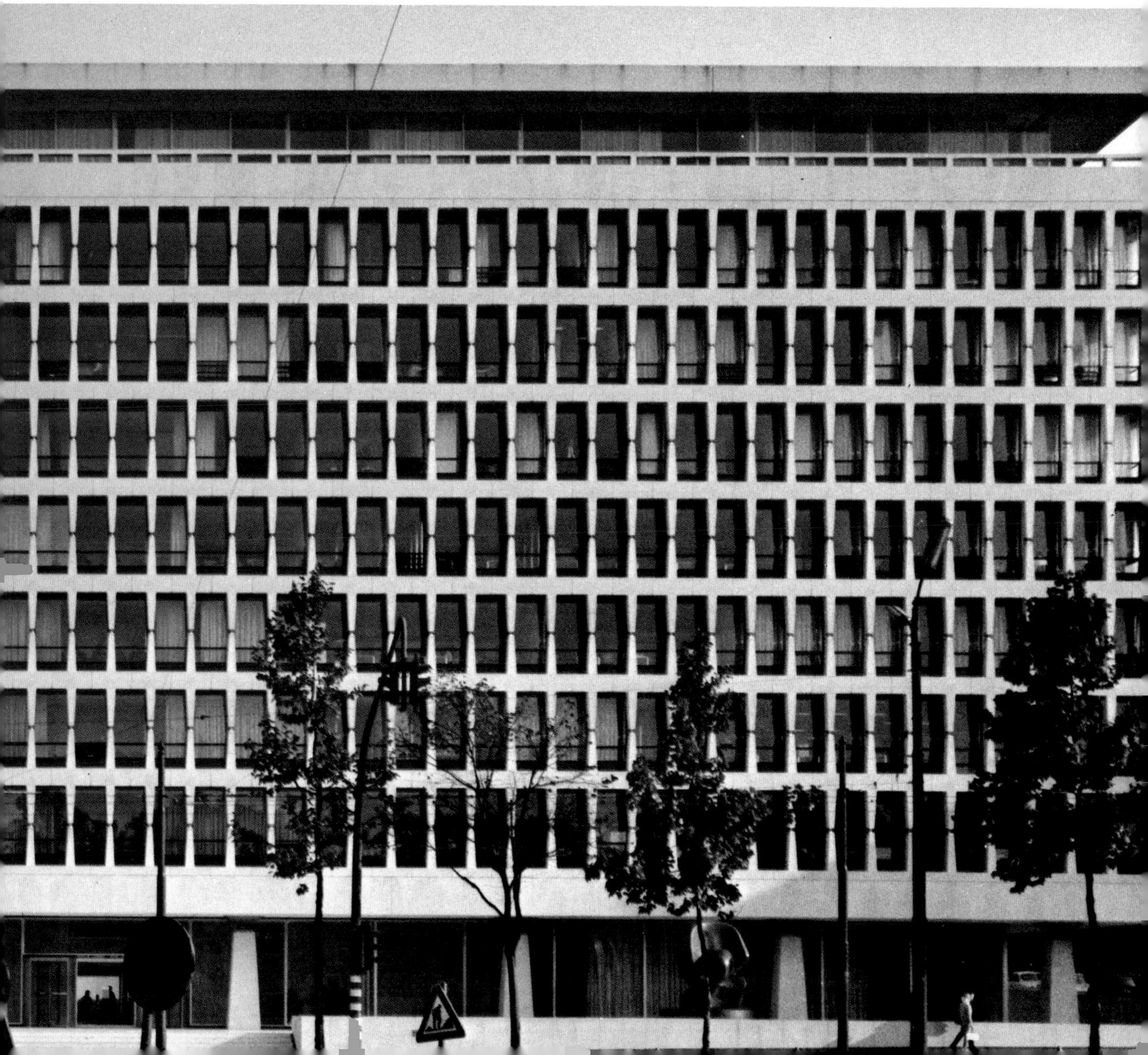

74-80, American Republic Insurance Company offices, Des Moines, Iowa (1965)

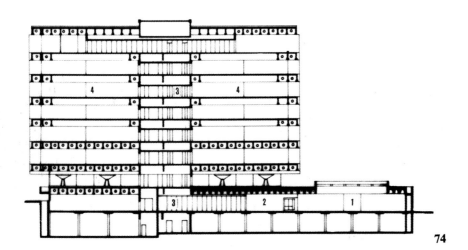

74

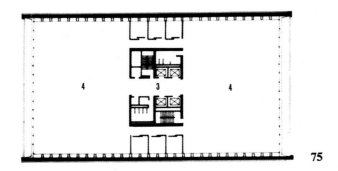

75

76

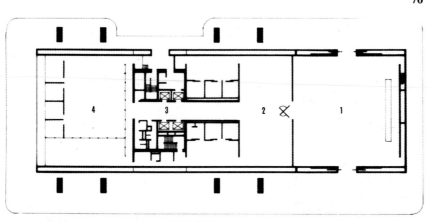

77

81-84, Beinecke Rare Book Room and Manuscript Library, Yale University, New Haven, Conn. (1960-63)

81, 82 Section (above), and plan of first floor: 1, exhibition hall; 2, book stack; 3, service core; 4, entrance hall; 5, plaza; 6, control desk; 7, basement book store

83 Long elevation to plaza

84 Exhibition niches and book-stack

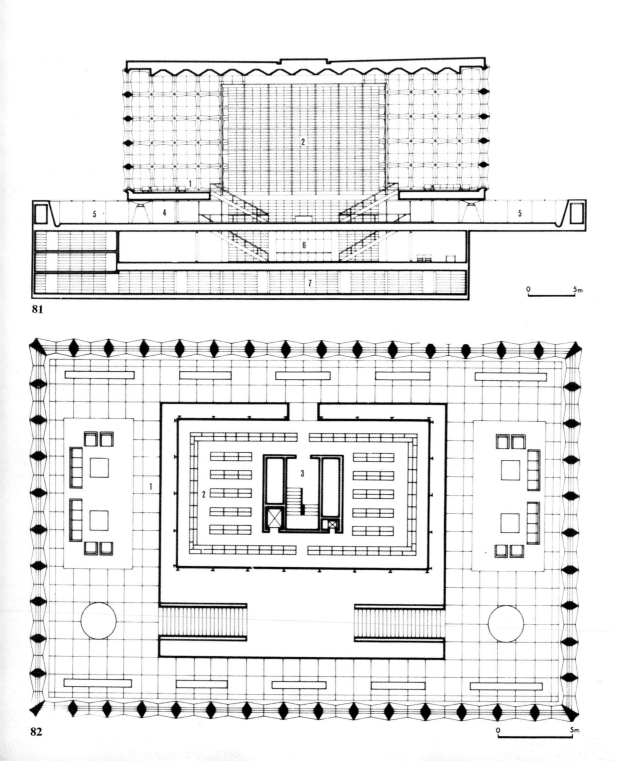

81

82

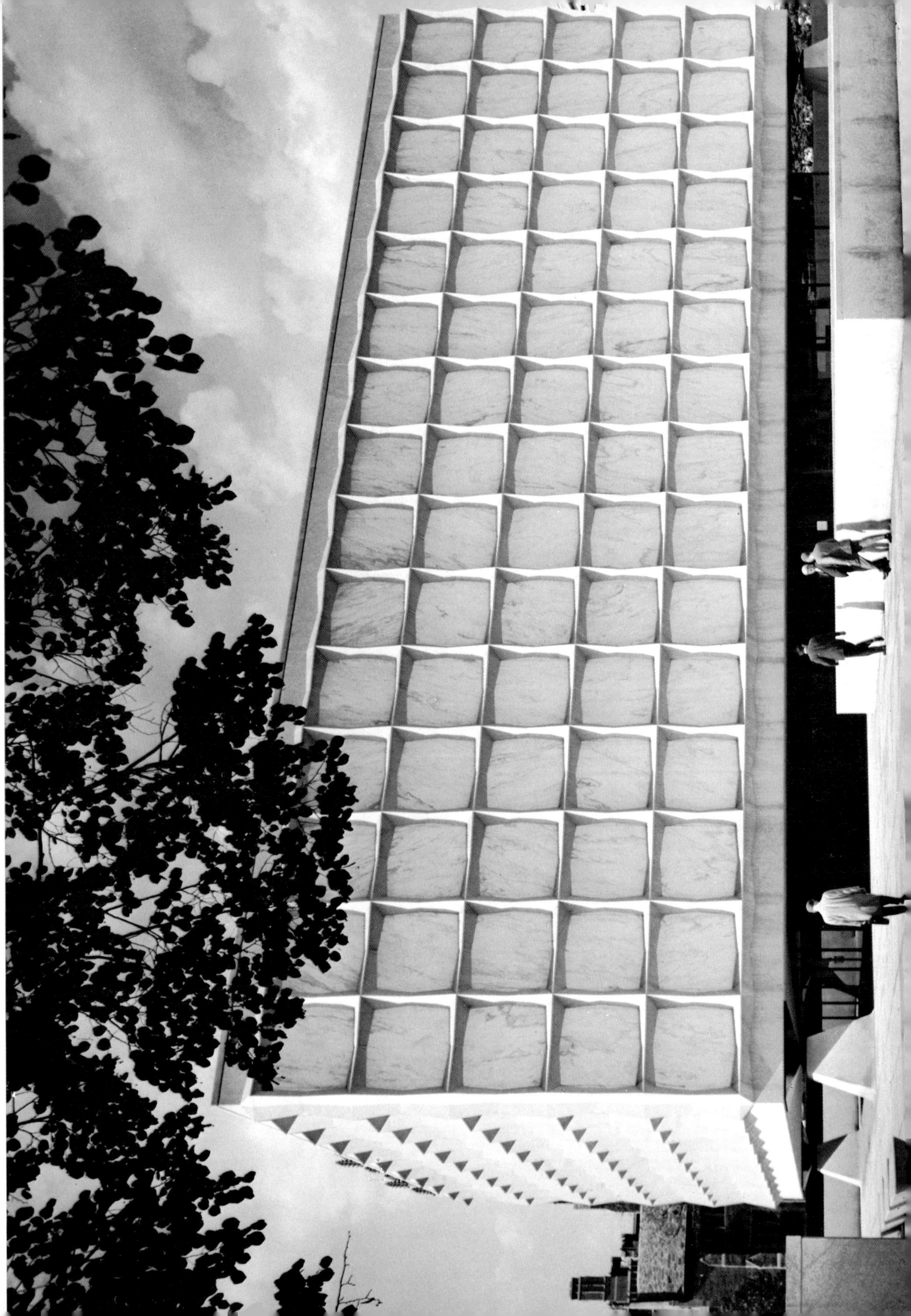

85-91, Mauna Kea Beach Hotel, Kaunaoa Bay, Hawaii (1965)

Charles Bassett

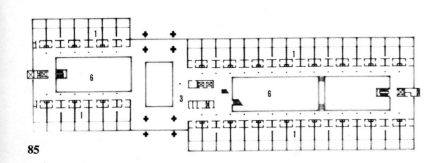

85

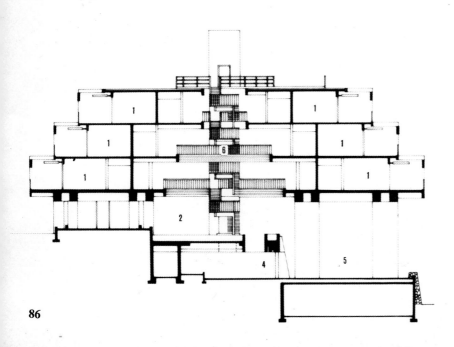

86

87

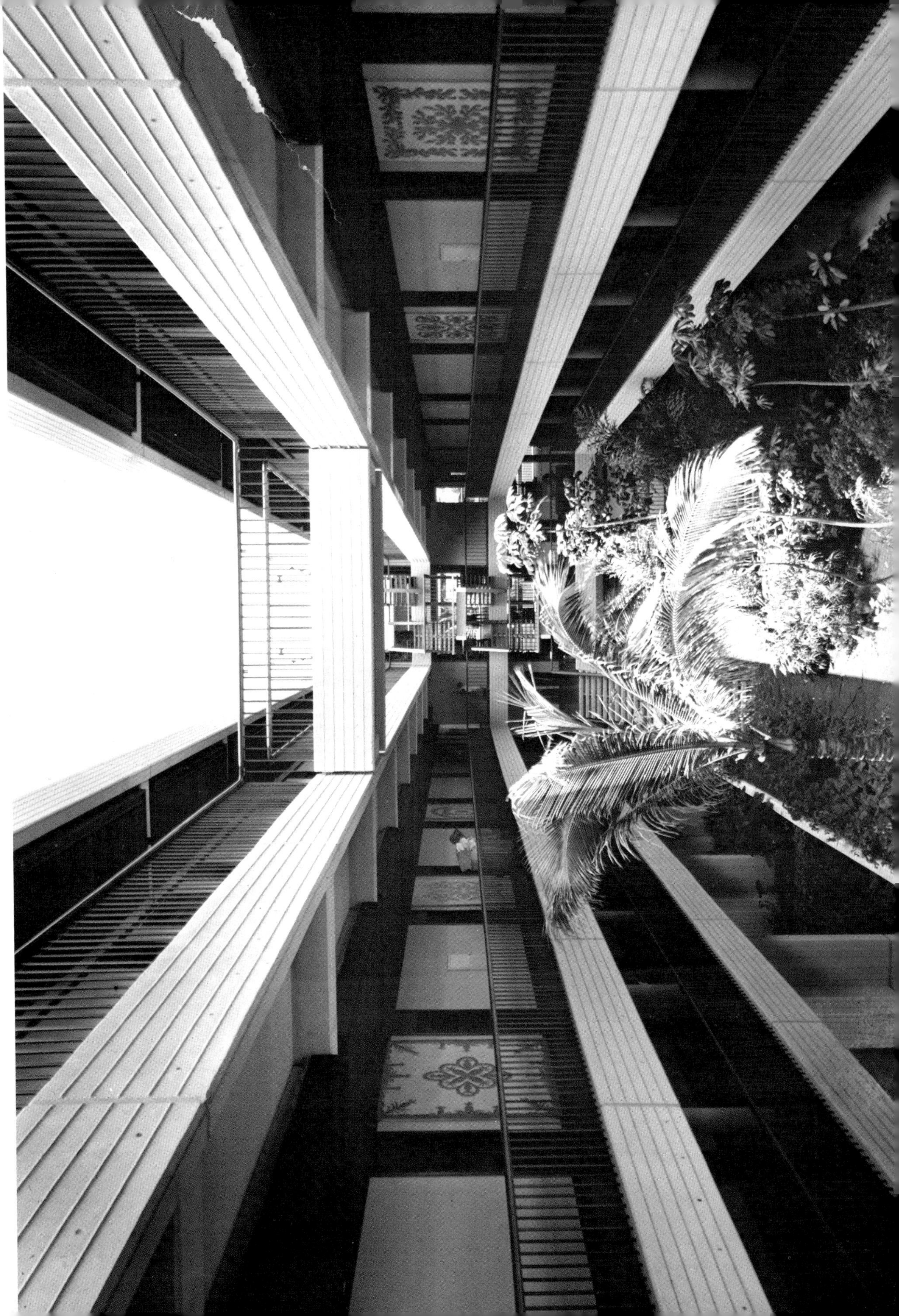

90, 91

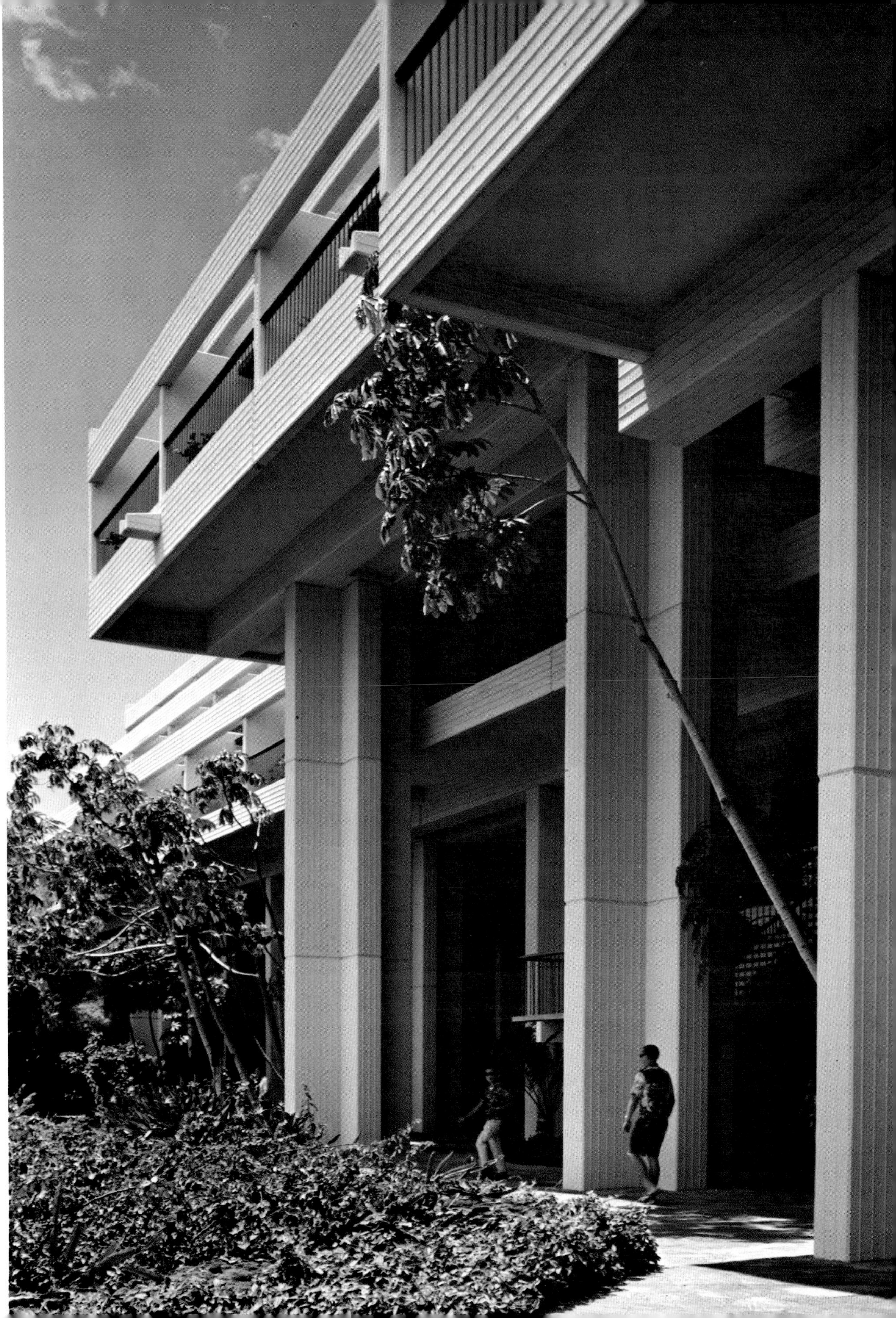

92-95, University of Illinois: Chicago campus (1965-   )

92 Site plan of the campus:
1, central plaza and amphitheatre;
2, pedestrian deck; 3, laboratories;
4, library; 5, student centre; 6,
administration tower; 7, arts
centre; 8, lecture rooms

93 Side elevation of administration building, showing progressive cantilevering of upper floors

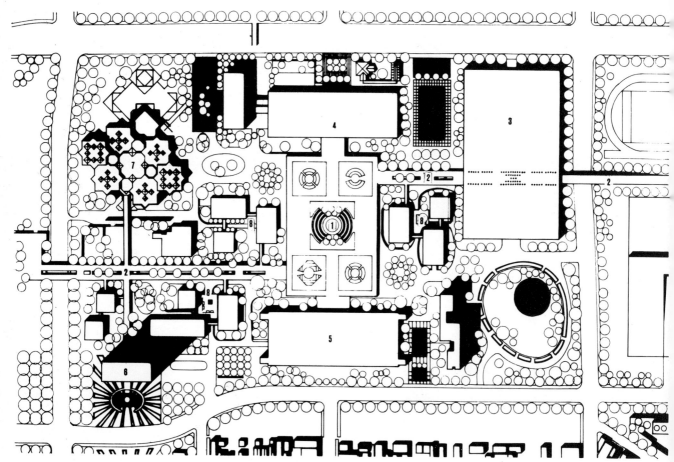

92

94 General view of administration tower

95 Central plaza and amphitheatre

**96-99, Brunswick Corporation offices,
Chicago, Ill. (1965)**

96

96 First-floor transfer truss and
ground-floor entrance lobby

97, 98 Plans of (left) ground floor,
and (right) typical office floor:
1, service core; 2, exhibition area;
3, 4, offices

99 General view (Civic Center at
left)

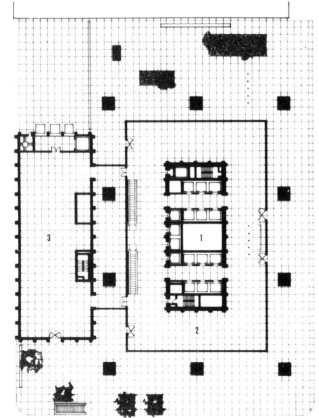

97

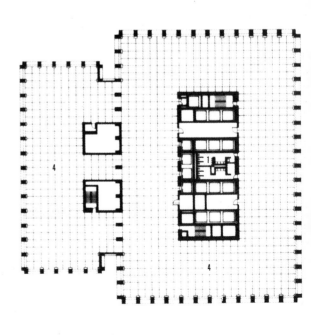

98

BUS STOP
22 CLARK
HALSTED-DOWNTOWN
42
ASHLAND-DOWNTOWN
CONESBURY

**100-105, Oakland-Alameda
County Coliseum,
Oakland, Calif. (1967)**

Charles Bassett

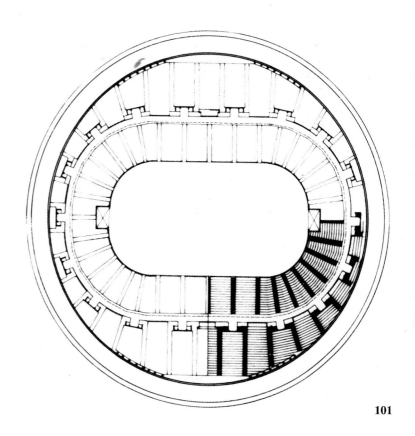

100 General view

101 Plan of covered stadium

102 Part section of covered
stadium

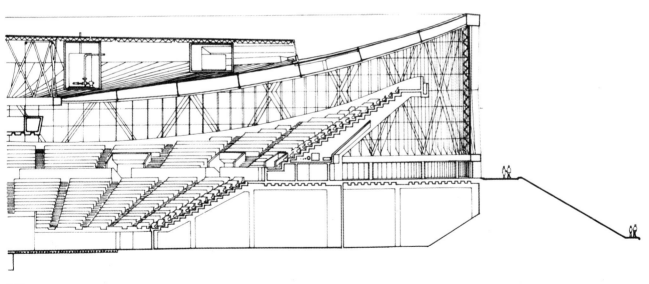

102

106-110, Hartford Fire Insurance Company offices, San Francisco, Calif. (1967)

106, 107 Site plan, and (left) typical office floor; A, St Mary's church; B, presbytery; C, Hartford building plaza. Key: 1, plaza; 2, entrance hall; 3, lift lobby; 4, cafeteria; 5, office space

108 General view from California Street

109 Plaza leading to recessed entrance hall

110 Detail of tower skin

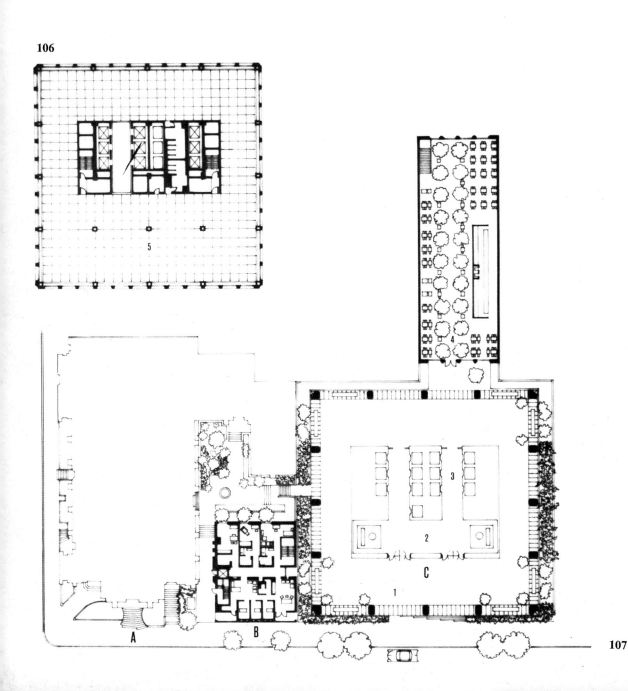

106

107

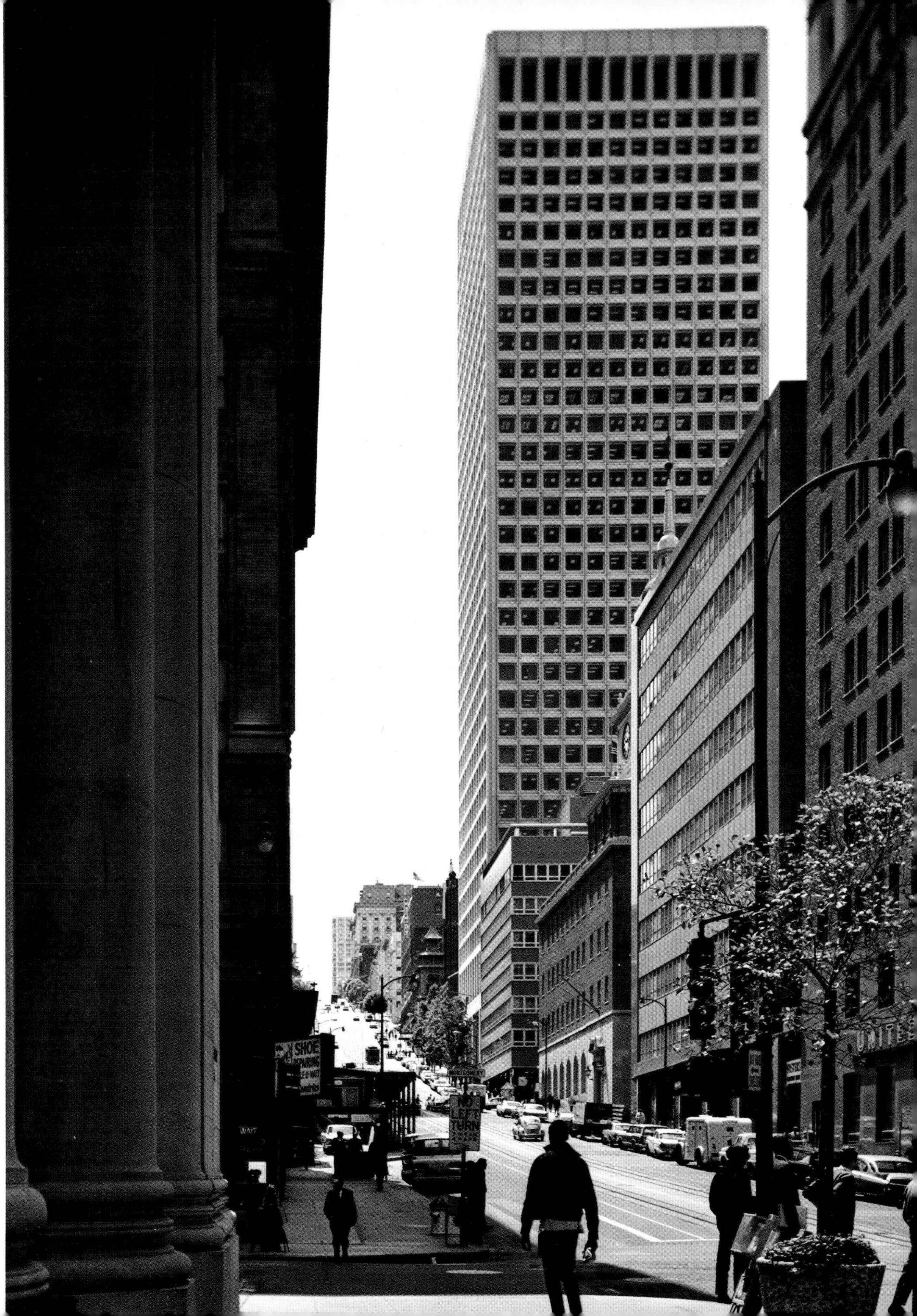
SHOE
MONTGOMERY
NO LEFT TURN
WAIT

**111-116, Alcoa Corporation offices, Golden Gate Center,
San Francisco, Calif. (1968)**

Charles Bassett

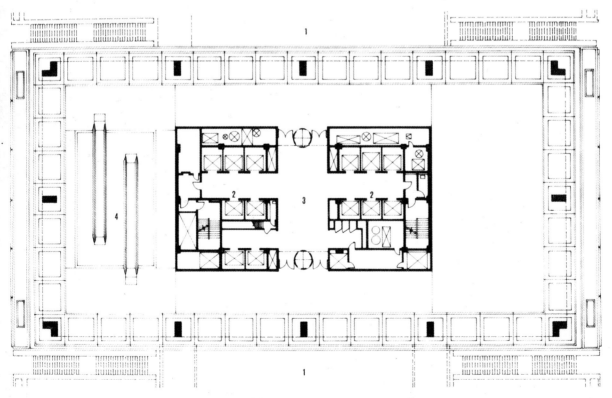

Notes on the plates

1-6
Lever House, Park Avenue,
New York (1951–52)

A 21-storey office tower, with plant rooms on top and service cores at the west end, is placed on a two-storey podium housing larger offices round a court open to the sky. The pavement level, except for the entrance hall, is open to the street. The first floor of the tower is set back and contains a dining room opening onto the landscaped roof of the podium. The skin is of green and transparent glass in 16 and 18 gauge stainless-steel frames, flush except for projecting mullions marking the columns behind.

7-11
Manufacturers Hanover Trust
Company branch bank,
Fifth Avenue, New York
(1953–54)

The branch building has four principal storeys, penthouse offices set back from the main façade, and basement. Two public banking halls connected by escalator occupy the ground and first floors, the lower containing the vault whose stainless-steel door can be seen from the pavement, and the upper a 70-ft long mural by Bertoia in bronzed sheet steel. There are two full floors and one half floor of offices over, and the basement houses mechanical equipment and staff accommodation. All levels have full illuminated ceilings of ribbed plastic sheets. The structure is of two rows of four steel columns carrying cantilevered concrete floor slabs, and the building is clad in projecting box-section aluminium mullions and transoms. The half-inch thick glass to the first-floor windows measures 9 ft 6 in. × 22 ft.

12–14
Inland Steel Company
headquarters building,
West Monroe St, Chicago, Ill.
(1956–58)

SOM's first post-war high building is an exercise in the separation of clear office space and service stacks. The headquarters of Inland Steel has nineteen office floors each of 10,000 square feet uninterrupted by structure. Mechanical plant is housed in three basement levels and in the top of the service stack. The fireproofed steel columns of the offices stand outside the skin and support beams, spanning 60 ft, and steel decking floors. Projecting window mullions, which also serve as cleaning-cradle guides, and transoms, spandrels, column cladding and the blind walls of the service tower, are of stainless steel.

15–17
Pepsi-Cola Company offices,
Park Avenue, New York
(1958–59)

Flanked by masonry street blocks, the 10-storey Pepsi-Cola building occupies a corner site. It is made to appear separate from its neighbours by a flash-gap wall clad in black granite, behind which the service functions are ranged along the party wall. The recessed ground-floor entrance hall, open to the public, is used for travelling exhibitions. Steel columns carry concrete floors illuminated at the perimeter. Silver aluminium mullions with tees project from an otherwise flush skin of half-inch glass; the spandrels are also of aluminium. Sun control is provided by travelling and vertically pivoting blinds.

18–25
U.S. Air Force Academy,
Colorado Springs, Col.
(1956–62)

The academy is a campus of teaching, residential and welfare buildings for 8,000 people, set on a platform 6,500 feet up in the Rockies. Buildings are separated by function: cadet housing, with an open access deck and set round courts, is on one edge of the platform, with the library and classroom block on the other. Between the arms of this L, and to one side, are the dining hall, the Court of Honor, two-level chapel, and social centre and sports hall. Motor traffic is restricted to a lower level. The buildings generally are clad in aluminium and glass, and have a variety of structures housing the disparate functions.

26, 27
Gunners' Mates School,
Great Lakes, Illinois (1952–54)

This 230-ft square building houses two teaching functions: two high practical demonstration areas, served by travelling cranes which handle guns and other weapons, are separated from each other by an internal central three-storey core of classrooms. The steel structure is of three 75-ft wide bays spanned by trusses, the middle one occupied by the core with its independent structure. Ventilation units are placed above the core; these draw air through opening lights at high and low levels in the skin, which is of industrial steel glazing sections and translucent blue-green glass.

28
H. J. Heinz Company,
Warehouse and Vinegar Plant,
Pittsburgh, Pennsylvania
(1950–52)

Two new industrial buildings, clad in contrasting materials, on an existing factory site are linked by a bridge. The first, a warehouse, is a concrete structure with mushroom-headed columns; it has a volume of eight million cubic feet and is clad in white glazed brick. The second (illustrated here) is an exposed steel-framed four-storey shed containing vinegar-processing vats. The glazed infill panels, of blue-green tinted glass, and opening lights have aluminium frames. The steel frame is painted black, the doors red.

29, 30
Connecticut General Life
Insurance Company
headquarters,
Bloomfield, Conn. (1954–57)

Three separate but linked buildings and two large open parking areas are disposed informally in a 280-acre landscaped park. The largest, the main office building, is of three storeys (two office floors above a ground floor devoted to social and staff welfare functions); it is 470 ft × 325 ft on plan, perforated by four 72-ft square landscaped courts between which are strips of service areas. A second three-storey office building houses small suites of single offices and is connected to the first by a bridge, and to a single-storey cafeteria by a wide enclosed link.

The planning module is 6 ft, with a structural bay size in the steel-framed main building of 72 ft × 60 ft. The three buildings are clad in aluminium curtain walls with blue-green transparent and opaque glazing.

31–36
Crown Zellerbach Corporation
headquarters building,
San Francisco, Calif. (1957–59)

Designed in association with Herzka and Knowles, this development occupies a triangular site on which are disposed a 20-storey office tower with clear floors served by a detached services stack, and a Wells Fargo branch bank in a circular pavilion. The ground areas remaining slightly below pavement level are heavily scalloped and landscaped. The visible structure of the tower shows no special earthquake precautions, fireproofed steel columns outside the floor space carrying rigid trusses which support the floor decking. The columns are supported at sub-basement level on a single concrete raft. The offices have a skin of aluminium box-section mullions at 5 ft 6 in. centres which hold green glass and master the spandrels. The offices are fitted-out using a movable partition system designed by SOM.

37–39

Union Carbide Corporation administrative offices, Park Avenue, New York (1957–60)

The office accommodation is arranged in a 52-storey tower, 707 feet high and rising straight from the pavement, linked to a twelve-storey 'bustle' facing away from Park Avenue. Each block is served by its own central core. Two levels of railway tracks which run under the site prevented full use of the basement, and lift pits are at ground level. The main circulation level is at the first floor, reached from the recessed entrance hall by a pair of escalators at ground level. The structure of steel columns is irregularly bayed because of the trains, but is based on a 2 ft 6 in. planning grid.

The building's skin and internal fittings make extensive use of both silver and black stainless steel. On the exterior the silver-coloured mullions pass the black steel cladding of floor edges and columns.

The interiors are entirely by SOM. On every floor there are complex illuminated ceilings divided up into 5 ft × 2 ft 6 in. rectangles, flush except for hangars which support the heads of the movable partitions. The tops of these partitions have a strip of glazing which enables the ceiling to be seen carrying across the office floors. All floors are carpeted.

40, 41

Harris Trust and Savings Bank offices, Chicago, Ill. (1957–60)

The newer 23-storey office tower occupying a whole Chicago block is connected to an older office building (which was renovated as part of the job) by a service stack. Mechanical plant for the new building is housed in the recessed eleventh and twelfth floors, and serves both upper and lower floors, leaving the basement free for vaults and the roof free for executive reception rooms grouped round a small courtyard. The steel-framed structure, with 20 ft × 25 ft bays, is clad in stainless steel with mullions at the planning grid centres of 5 ft.

42–45

First City National Bank branch bank and offices, Houston, Texas (1959–61)

Designed by SOM's New York office in association with Wilson, Morris, Crain and Anderson, the single-storey branch bank to which the public have access both on foot and by car is linked to a 32-storey office tower on one block. A parking building on a diagonally adjacent block serves both buildings by a subway. The tower, the top three storeys of which accommodate plant, has a central service core and three by nine bay steel-frame structure cased in concrete. Neoprene-beaded grey glass is held in steel-reinforced aluminium frames set back behind the external structural frame which is faced in white Vermont marble. The branch bank has a single-span steel structure, is 34 feet high and, when built, had the longest teller-counter in the U.S.A. The suspended ceiling of 914 champagne-coloured aluminium pyramids, each holding a light, covers the whole space.

46–50

Tennessee Gas Building Corporation offices, Houston, Texas (1964)

This building, by the SOM San Francisco office, is a 33-storey office tower, 575 feet high; occupying an entire city block, it has a plan 170 feet square, and a spirally symmetrical core. A recessed two-storey banking hall occupies the first and second floors, and mechanical plant the ninth and twenty-fifth. The structural frame is covered with bronze anodised aluminium, and the clip-on horizontal sunbreaks, and recessed glazing framing, with mullions at 5 ft 6 in. centres, are made of the same bronze anodised aluminium.

51–56
Chase Manhattan Bank offices, New York (1957–61)

Two city blocks in the Wall Street area were combined to produce a 2¼-acre site, nearly three-quarters of which, not occupied by the office tower, forms a roof over the first basement, and is made over for pedestrian use. The 60-storey office tower, 250×100 ft on plan, has an off-centre service core and the perimeter columns of cased steel are set outside the perimeter glazing of silver anodised aluminium mullions and spandrels. The columns are covered in aluminium sheet. Under the plaza, a public concourse from one side of the block to the other gives access to a banking hall which looks onto a circular court open to the sky and decorated with cobbles and stones by Isamu Noguchi.

57–64
Upjohn Company headquarters offices, Kalamazoo, Mich. (1959–61)

The 432-ft square one-storey building is on a slightly sloping rural site of 100 acres. A continuous basement runs under the whole of the building proper, occasionally looking onto one of the courts (of varying size and landscape treatment) which punctuate the plan. The visible structure is of aluminium-covered steel columns at 48 ft centres supporting the two-way spanning space frame which houses the air-conditioning trunking and plaster lighting coffers. At its perimeter, the frame is enclosed by aluminium cladding. Double glazing is held in aluminium frames. Internally, subdivision is by fully movable partitions on a 6 ft module.

65–69
Emhart Manufacturing Company administration and research building, Bloomfield, Conn. (1963)

Another 100-acre country site (near Connecticut General Life Insurance's offices of 1954–57) provided the setting for 160,000 square feet of office, laboratory and service space. The single main floor is supported above ground level on *pilotis* with ribbed mushroom caps forming bays 42 ft square. General office space surrounds two areas, one a core of laboratories with its own separate structure, the other an open court whose floor forms the roof of the basement housing parking space and mechanical equipment. Precast concrete columns standing on the edges of the floor deck support a steel roof trimmed with precast eaves.

70–73
Banque Lambert, Brussels (1964)

An eight-storey office slab, 100×240 ft on plan, with a ninth recessed floor of flats, is set on a podium which covers two basement floors, occupying a complete block. The office structure is of precast crosses butt-jointed at each floor-slab level but connected at the mid-point between floors by stainless-steel pin-joints. The loads from these frames are collected on a beam at first-floor level, and transferred on to tapered columns set back from the main façade; behind these columns is the banking hall. The offices are not fully air-conditioned, but the glazing skin with its opening lights is recessed.

74–80
American Republic Insurance Company offices, Des Moines, Iowa (1965)

Five office floors with recessed glazed ends are supported through pin-joints onto eight, large concrete columns at ground level. Each of the five office floors has an area clear of columns on either side of a service core. There are no suspended ceilings and the spaces between the concrete beams spanning from crosswall to crosswall are used to house diffused lighting troughs and, near the windows, air-conditioning ducts.

Beinecke Rare Book and
Manuscript Library,
Yale University,
New Haven, Conn. (1960–63)

The library, which is set back from the pavement edge of its block, stands in an area of close-packed university buildings. The main building, raised above an entrance lobby, houses a detached air-conditioned bookstack and display cases. The basement level contains reading rooms and librarian's offices which look onto an open court with sculptures by Noguchi.

The structure of the elevated 'case' consists of steel-framed Vierendel trusses made up of cross elements, tapered in both directions and faced with stone. Glazing between the trusses is of translucent alabaster. The wall trusses are supported at ground level on four set-back concrete columns, the connexions made with pin-joints.

85–91
Manna Kea Beach Hotel,
Kaunaoa Bay, Hawaii (1965)

The low-lying building stands close to the seashore, parallel to the beach; the hotel has 138 bedrooms arranged on three floors. Each storey is set back on the outside faces to provide balconies. Access to the rooms is from open galleries round courts, and the entire structure is carried on ribbed reinforced-concrete *pilotis* which allow the beach vegetation to spread under the building into the courts. The dining rooms and other central facilities are also accommodated at ground-floor level.

92–95
University of Illinois:
Chicago campus (1965)

Designed in conjunction with C. F. Murphy Associates, A. Epstein and Sons, the campus is situated next to the intersection of the Kennedy and Eisenhower expressways. It occupies 100 acres and will eventually serve 14,000 students and graduates in a variety of buildings, mainly of concrete construction, loosely grouped round a central plaza with a circular amphitheatre; from the corners of the plaza two elevated walkways run north and south. The 27-storey administration tower, with its progressively further cantilevering upper floors, and exposed rough-boarded *in situ* structural frame, is the tallest building on the Chicago campus.

96–99
Brunswick Corporation offices,
Chicago, Ill. (1965)

On a corner site facing the Civic Center, this 35-storey, 500-ft high office building has a figure-of-eight plan form: a main office area with central core, connected with a neck to an open 'bustle'. The reinforced-concrete structure has closely spaced (9 ft 4 in. centres) columns collected onto an outward-flaring beam, one storey in height, behind which plant is housed. The beam is carried by ten travertine-covered columns, 9 feet square, at pavement level.

100–105
Oakland-Alameda County
Coliseum, Oakland, Calif.
(1967)

Two circular stadia, one covered and one open, are linked by administrative offices, and together provide a comprehensive, multi-purpose flexible sports centre. The covered stadium has an external diameter of 770 ft, and the roof construction employs radial suspension cables spanning between and across concrete compression ring-beams, the outer one supported on concrete X-shaped columns placed outside the fully glazed skin. Ventilation plant is housed over the centre of the roof, and is supported by it.

106–110
Hartford Fire Insurance
Company offices,
San Francisco, Calif. (1967)

A square-planned, 35-storey office tower with a central service core is fitted on to a small sloping site in downtown San Francisco. The structure is of smooth-finished reinforced concrete; columns closely spaced are collected at plaza level on to more widely spaced ones which mark out a small plaza formed by deeply recessing the entrance hall. A single-storey staff cafeteria opens off this plaza.

111–116
Alcoa Corporation offices,
Golden Gate Center,
San Francisco, Calif. (1968)

Part of an urban redevelopment of twenty acres, the Alcoa offices stand above a two-storey car-parking podium, the roof of which is landscaped and decorated. The tower, which rises 26 storeys above the podium, has a central service core; the external vertical structure, the diagonal wind- and earthquake-bracing and the spandrels are clad in bronze anodised aluminium. The brown-glass windows are in similar aluminium frames.

Chronological list: events and projects

Buildings are listed under date of completion unless otherwise stated.

1897 Louis Skidmore born in Indiana

1903 Nathaniel Owings born in Indiana

1933 Skidmore and Owings work on designs for Chicago exposition

1936 Partnership formed between Skidmore and Owings

1937 New York branch office opened under Skidmore; Gordon Bunshaft joins firm

1939 John Merrill brought into partnership as structural engineer

1942–46 Work on 'Atom City', Oak Ridge, Tennessee; recreation and welfare buildings for Great Lakes Training Center, Illinois

1946 Bunshaft, William Brown, Robert Cutler and Walter Severinghaus become partners

1949–50 Lake Meadows housing project, Chicago, Ill.; Terrace Plaza Hotel, Cincinnati, Ohio; Brooklyn Hospital, New York

1950 Basis for office organization set up by Owings

1952 Lever House, Park Avenue, New York; Heinz vinegar plant and warehouse, Pittsburgh, Pa

1954 Manufacturers Hanover Trust, Fifth Avenue Branch, New York; Gunners Mates School, Great Lakes, Illinois

1954–55 U.S. Consulate, Dusseldorf, and housing for U.S. State Department, Bremen, West Germany

1957 Connecticut General Life Insurance offices, Bloomfield, Conn.

1958 Myron Goldsmith joins San Francisco office; Reynolds Metals Company, Richmond, Va; United Air Lines hangars, San Francisco Airport; Inland Steel headquarters, Chicago, Ill.

1959 Goldsmith moves to Chicago office; John Hancock Mutual Life Insurance building, San Francisco; Crown Zellerbach offices, San Francisco; Pepsi-Cola building, Park Avenue, New York

1960 Union Carbide building, Park Avenue, New York; Harris Trust and Savings building, Chicago, Ill.

1961 Chase Manhattan Bank, New York; Upjohn Pharmaceuticals Company, Kalamazoo, Michigan; First City National Bank, Houston, Texas

1962 U.S. Air Force Academy, Colorado Springs; United Air Lines offices, Des Plaines, Ill.

1963 Emhart Manufacturing offices, Bloomfield, Conn.; Beinecke Library, Yale University, New Haven, Conn.

1964 Banque Lambert, Brussels headquarters; Tennessee Gas Building Corporation main offices, Houston, Texas

1965 American Republic Insurance Company, Des Moines, Iowa; Brunswick Corporation offices, Chicago, Ill.; Mauna Kea Beach Hotel, Hawaii; University of Illinois, Chicago Campus

1967 Oakland-Alameda County Coliseum, Oakland, Calif.; Hartford Fire Insurance Company, San Francisco, Calif.

1968 John Hancock Center, Chicago, Ill.; Alcoa offices, Golden Gate Center, San Francisco, Calif.

Bibliographical note

The only large book on SOM's work is Ernst Danz, *Architecture of Skidmore, Owings & Merrill, 1950–1962*, London, 1963. The fullest descriptions of the individual buildings to be found elsewhere have appeared in reviews in the American technical press, to which the entries for SOM in the Avery Index to Architectural Periodicals, Columbia University, New York, provides an apparently exhaustive guide.

Two articles warrant separate mention: for a description of the growth of the firm, see *Fortune*, January 1958; for a view of SOM seen from England in relation to American culture, see Peter Smithson, 'The Fine and the Folk', *Architectural Design*, August 1965.

Offices and personnel

The details listed below are taken from *SOM Handbook*, November 1968.

Skidmore, Owings & Merrill
Architects and Engineers

Offices	*Personnel*	
New York, N.Y. 10022 400 Park Avenue	General Partners	19
	Associate Partners	41
Chicago, Illinois 60603 30 West Monroe Street	Project Managers	30
San Francisco, California 94111 One Maritime Plaza	Research, Programming, Reports	5
	Plan Directors	5
Portland, Oregon 97204 1100 S.W. Sixth Avenue	City Planners	15
	Site Planners	10
	Chiefs of Design	4
	Designers	203
	Interior Designers	35
	Chiefs of Production	4
	Draftsmen	230
	Landscape Architects	5
	Architectural Engineers	10
	Structural Engineers	34
	Mechanical Engineers	86
	Electrical Engineers	41
	Civil Engineers	3
	Estimators	12
	Specification Writers	16
	Chiefs of Construction	4
	Construction Superintendents	51
	Office Management, Secretarial, Computers, Accountants	157
	Total	1,020

Index